# Taking Refuge
## *Lao Buddhists in North America*

*Penny Van Esterik*

Monographs in Southeast Asian Studies
Program for Southeast Asian Studies
Arizona State University

Editor: Mark Woodward
Layout: Stephen Toth
Copy Editor: Sally Bennett
Cover Design: Sheila Johns
National Resource Undergraduate Center Director:
Juliane Schober

This publication funded in part by the
U. S. Department of Education

ISBN# 1-881044-04-1

# Acknowledgments

It is a pleasure to thank some of the individuals who have made this publication possible. During the research, I was ably assisted by Sasichome Xoomsai, with occasional assistance from other Thai students at York University. I am most grateful to Bruce Matthews, Louis-Jacques Dorais and anonymous reviewers for catching some of my worst blunders and making excellent suggestions for revisions.

I acknowledge with regret that I have not been able to explore topics of ethnic identity and Buddhist practice in Laos in more detail. The book began with the simple goal of introducing Lao refugees and Buddhism into the literature of refugee studies, without the historical, legal, theological, linguistic and anthropological footnotes that could accompany this task. I have attempted to use the most common transcriptions for Pali, Thai and Lao terms, and I am grateful to those who have improved these transcriptions for me.

I want to thank the Joint Centre for Asia Pacific Studies for initially funding the project and the York Centre for Refugee Studies and the Program for Southeast Asian Studies at Arizona State University for copublishing the volume. The efforts of Howard Adelman (CRS) and Mark Woodward (ASU) are much appreciated, and I look forward to continued collaboration between the two institutions.

This project grew out of my respect for and interest in Lao Buddhism and the Lao refugees who have struggled to maintain their traditions in North America. To the Lao people who have welcomed me to their services and their lives, I offer my sincere thanks. And to my husband, John, whose knowledge of Buddhism, refugees and me enriched this work, my thanks and my love.

# Contents

## Chapter 7  Buddhism and Mental Health

# List of Tables

# Chapter One

## Introduction

### Raising the Curtain

*Fa Ngum, after having put these provinces in good order, brought back his soldiers towards the Lan Xang and stopped at Vieng Chan (Vientiane). . .the whole people raised their hands to the King, saying: "You have made us great, proud and victorious over other countries. We thank you and wish to raise you once again to the throne of Lan Xang."*

*The Phra Chao Fa Ngum, having heard the people and his warriors speak thus, replied: "You speak thus, I am pleased, I accept."At once the whole Sena-Amat set about preparing the ceremony on the site later occupied by the Wat Passac (Royal Temple). When this was finished, they came to fetch the King, and during seven days and seven nights, there was feasting in the Palace and among the people. They killed 10 elephants, 1000 oxen and 2000 buffaloes which were to be carefully prepared for the table. Then the King spoke thus to the chiefs, in the presence of the army and the people who had come along by all the rivers:*

*"You will attend to all the usual practices and administer justice in the Lan Xang; see to it that there are no pirates, thieves, murderers or rebels. See to it that the masters are kind to their slaves, that they do not strike them but forgive them their evil ways. If any chiefs or their children behave badly or are unjust, the chief who arrests them must submit them to the decision of other judges so that he himself may not be suspected of being unjust. The guilty ones must be punished according to their offenses and released from prison on the day fixed by the judge so that they may return to their families and try to live with them once again. In the country there are rich and poor alike. Everyone must accept his station in life so that we may never have to condemn anyone to death. If enemies from abroad form evil designs against the country, as soon as these things come to your knowledge, give warning and do not keep such grave news to yourselves."*

*The great coronation ceremonies were renewed so that the King's reign might be long-lasting and the King and Queen might have beautiful children and the peoples be as happy in the future as they were then. After conquering so many provinces, the King Fa Ngum had come back to the country to enjoy a rest.* (de Berval 1959:397–399)

This myth can only open the curtain to reveal the culture and life of a people (cf. Daniel 1984:233) if the reader knows something about the Kingdom of Lan Xang, Prince Fa Ngum and the country of Laos in Southeast Asia. But the myth has meaning for thousands of lowland Lao who left their country as refugees in large numbers in the late 1970s. To share their stories and understand who they are, we need to know something of their history and myths and the religion that structured their lives.

Laos is a small, landlocked country of approximately four million people surrounded by Burma, Thailand, Cambodia, Vietnam and China. One of the poorest and most rural countries in Asia even before its revolution and involvement in the Indochina war, it has spent the last decade struggling to create a self-sufficient socialist state, while rebuilding an economy almost totally destroyed by French colonial rule and saturation bombing by the United States in the late 1960s. About two million tons of bombs hit the country between 1965 and 1975, making Laos one of the most intensively bombed countries in the world.

Since the fourteenth century, lowland Lao and the upland peoples have been integrated into a number of ethnically stratified Buddhist states ruled by powerful princes. The loose union of princedoms was brought about by Prince Fa Ngum upon his return from exile in Cambodia (around 1350), where he married the daughter of the Cambodian king. The Cambodian king armed his son-in-law and helped Fa Ngum claim the throne at Luang Prabang, later the royal capital of Laos. Victorious over lesser lords, Fa Ngum named his state Lan Xang (Land of a Million Elephants) and began to wage war against local princes who refused to recognize his authority. Lan Xang spread beyond what is now Laos into parts of what are now Thailand, Cambodia, Vietnam and China. Fa Ngum and his wife asked the king of Cambodia for "religion," since, they said, the people of Lan Xang do not know much about religion. In 1358, a Khmer Buddhist mission arrived from Cambodia bringing learned monks, Buddhist texts and the palladium of Laos, the Prabang Buddha image. For the next four centuries, Laos was ruled by a series of rulers who alternately allied with and fought the Vietnamese and the Siamese. As Lan Xang prospered even the Burmese invaded the kingdom, eventually taking hostages and disrupting royal power. By 1700 the first Europeans visited the country and found not one but three rival kingdoms: Vientiane, Luang Prabang and Champassak. Weakened by Siamese invasions beginning in the 1770s, the Kingdom of Vientiane became part of the Siamese kingdom by 1829, and the Prabang palladium was taken to Bangkok, only to be returned in 1867 by Mongkut, King of Thailand. France gradually increased her control over Vietnam and viewed control over the Lao kingdoms as a way to protect Vietnam's western borders. By the nineteenth century Lan Xang was reduced to a number of princedoms easily captured by the French in 1893, ending Thai domination of the country. By the Franco-Siamese treaty of 1893, Siam recognized France's control of the left bank of the Mekong River, and the remnants of the Kingdom of Lan Xang became a French Protectorate (de Berval 1959; Coedès 1968 ). Its demise as a powerful empire can be explained:

> The landlocked kingdoms of mainland Southeast Asia some 600 years ago depended on land trade between China and India and places in between for their wealth. When the Europeans began shifting the major trade routes to the world's seas, the only nations that could grow economically and politically were those with access to the sea. Thailand, through its port capital at Bangkok, survived the European onslaught and grew in power, whereas Laos, landlocked and with its capital on a river not navigable to the sea, shrank in power and extent. (J. Van Esterik 1985:151)

The French allowed the Lao king to keep his royal prerogatives and palace in Luang Prabang, while the French resident developed Vientiane, the present capital of the Lao People's Democratic Republic, as the administrative capital. Throughout colonial rule, the French undermined the Buddhist moral order and did virtually nothing to develop industry, education, or any other Lao institution. The first secular school in Laos was established in 1907 to train interpreters needed by the French (Luangpraseut 1989:18). Laos obtained its independence from France in 1954, but only after substantial confrontation and confusion. During this time, the Pathet Lao, with the assistance of Ho Chi Minh's Vietnamese communist troops, extended their influence throughout Laos. After Saigon and Phnom Penh collapsed in 1975, the communist Pathet Lao took control of the Lao People's Democratic Republic. These events in brief set the stage for the exodus of Lao refugees into Thailand in the late 1970s, and on to North America by the 1980s.

This book discusses the least-known group of Indochinese refugees, the lowland Lao or Lao Loum, the ethnic group comprising about half the population of Laos. I use the term Lao to refer to the inhabitants and former inhabitants of lowland Laos, ignoring the complexities of the fact that the term is "constituted through the merging of legendary, historical, political, scholarly and popular discourses" (Rajah 1990:328). While media attention highlighted the experiences of the Vietnamese "boat people" and the survivors of Pol Pot's Khmer Rouge regime, very little scholarly attention has been focused on the third country contributing to the Southeast Asian refugee flow. There are few studies of the lowland Lao in North America. In studies of Southeast Asian refugees, Lao are often merged with Khmer or Vietnamese in such a way as to render them invisible in relation to the larger groups. Since 1975 when the Pathet Lao established the Lao People's Democratic Republic (LPDR), about ten percent of the population of one of the world's poorest countries left as refugees—including most of the skilled and schooled. Most Lao refugees came to North America, with over 15,000 settling in Canada.

This study of Lao refugee resettlement builds around the attempts of Lao communities to recreate their Buddhist institutions in North America. Lao refugees differ by age, gender, class, region of origin and political orientation. The institutions that crosscut many of these categories are Buddhist associations and Lao temples. Using data from Lao refugees in the Toronto area, this book explores the refugee experience through the practice of Lao Buddhism.

Why examine refugee adaptation through the perspective of religion? What could be accomplished by such an examination? First, I hope this study will be a useful resource for Lao resettled in North America who will take this opportunity to correct and expand on my version of their story. Second, I hope that this work will encourage the integration of Lao Buddhism into scholarship on Theravada Buddhism. In researching this book, references were scarce, to say the least. Third, perhaps this work will begin to redress the imbalance in refugee studies toward more cultural analysis and away from the refugee experience defined solely in political and legal terms. Religion is one basis for self and ethnic identity, and it is this identity that is often stripped away from refugees as they leave their homeland. Nevertheless, religion has been virtually ignored in studies of the adaptive process of refugee resettlement. Fourth, even for those not involved in refugee issues, Buddhism is a subject of great interest to North Americans. It is the fastest-growing religion in North America, yet we have few ways of accessing Buddhism as it is practiced by groups who were "born Buddhist," as opposed to those who learn Buddhism through teachers, texts or meditation training. The descriptions of how the Lao practice Buddhism should provide a "feel" for Buddhist practice in North America. This perspective on refugee adjustment is not meant to replace the more usual emphasis on economic integration, but rather to present an additional and often overlooked dimension. Finally, I hope this book opens new questions in refugee research. Some of these questions concern the meaning of cultural values and religious traditions as resources both for resettlement in countries of asylum and for repatriation, the transformation of Lao women's gender identity in North America, and the importance of understanding the meaning of loss of place and locality for refugees.

Following a discussion of my perspective on this research, details of the creation of the refugee flow, escape into Thailand, waiting in Thai camps and resettlement in North America are discussed in the second chapter. The third chapter places the Lao experience in the broader context of research on refugees and religion, with particular emphasis on prerevolutionary Buddhism in Laos, religion in the camp setting and the dilemmas emerging from religious support in camps and sponsorship in countries of third asylum.

At the heart of the book are the descriptions of Wat Lao (Lao temple) and the rituals it provides for Lao Buddhists in Toronto. Each ritual is described and analyzed based on participant observation in Toronto (Chapter Four). Chapter Five considers the relation of Wat Lao to other Buddhist groups in Toronto and North America.

Building on this descriptive base, Chapter Six analyzes the adaptive strategies transforming Buddhism as practiced in Laos to Buddhism as practiced in North America. The concluding chapter uses key Lao rituals—binding the soul to the body, extending merit to others and feeding monks—as metaphors for the survival strategies of Lao refugees in North America.

**Perspectives on the Research**

As an anthropologist specializing in mainland Southeast Asia, I was familiar with the work of anthropologists and historians on Laos. But as a Thai specialist, I am sure I overlooked Laos in much of my work on culture, history and religion. I reflect the bias of those who work with the more politically powerful of the Thai peoples and pay less attention to the "younger brothers" of the Thai (such as the Lao and the Shan) within the large language family of Tai speakers. This research provided an opportunity to redress imbalance. In 1985, I received seed funding from the Joint Centre for Modern East Asia (now the Joint Centre for Asia Pacific Studies) to carry out a small study of Theravada Buddhism among Lao and Khmer refugees in Toronto. The project began with telephone interviews and literature review to learn what Buddhist resources existed in Toronto. From initial interviews and participation in a wide range of Buddhist services, I quickly learned that the resources were so substantial that it would be necessary to limit the research to one group, the Lao. My background in Thai Studies prepared me for work on Lao religion, but it would be an exaggeration to claim expertise on the complexities of Lao history or on immigration and refugee policy. Like many Southeast Asianists, my husband—also an anthropologist trained in Thai Studies—and I became drawn to refugee issues not through research but through advocacy work on behalf of Southeast Asian refugees in North America. We were resources for orientations and workshops run by service providers rushing to find out something about

Southeast Asia. Faced with an unprecedented flood of refugees from Vietnam, Laos and Cambodia in 1979 and 1980, they sought expertise on these countries, and we willingly provided it, amazed to find that our esoteric knowledge within anthropology was extremely useful to those who wanted to sponsor and assist refugees from Southeast Asia.(cf. P. Van Esterik 1980a) Although my husband had developed programs for refugees, much of my subjective understanding of refugees grew from the experience of sponsoring a family of Cambodian refugees who lived with us for several months. The intensity of this experience fueled my commitment to refugee research, and although the family does not appear anywhere in this research, they are at the same time everywhere.

Another level of understanding came from brief visits to Laos in 1968 and 1990. In the latter trip I was able to visit temples and participate in services in Vientiane after having researched the same services among Lao refugees in Toronto. In addition to interviewing some key informants in Laos, I also had an opportunity to visit several refugee camps in Thailand and interview both refugees and service providers informally.

Most of this research is based on participant observation of Lao ritual events in Toronto held from 1986 to 1990 and on participation in a limited number of other Buddhist services. Throughout the research period I was assisted by John Van Esterik and Sasichome Xoomsai, along with the occasional assistance of Thai students. In addition to this participant observation, I conducted a small survey of those attending Buddhist services in Toronto.

The service marking the end of the rains retreat or Buddhist "Lent" (Ok Phansa) was celebrated in a community hall on Sunday, October 18, 1987. With permission from the Lao Association of Ontario and the Lao Buddhist Association, I distributed a survey to the Lao attending that service. Before the service began, the head of the Lao Buddhist Association explained that I was writing a report on Lao Buddhism and wanted to ask some questions about their religious practices. Since my husband and I had attended many services in the past, they were prepared to trust us on this occasion after the purpose was explained. The Lao were well aware of the fact that Canadians know very little about Buddhism. The leaders of the Lao Association knew that if Canadians had any interest in Buddhism, it was probably Japanese Zen or Tibetan Mahayana Buddhism. In the three years I attended services, there were no Canadian sponsors attending services. Recently, a few Lao teenagers have occasionally brought Canadian teenaged friends to services. The Lao permitted my intrusion because they are extraordinarily patient and tolerant people and because it was important to some of them that Canadians learn something of their religious traditions.

Having said that, I must also acknowledge the context that makes this far from a scientific survey. It is not representative of the Lao in Toronto, but rather of a very special group of Lao who regularly attend Buddhist services when they are conducted in Toronto. The questions focused on religion, with some background questions on their experiences as refugees and their education and occupation in Canada. I prepared a set of questions in English and translated them roughly into Thai to judge how they would sound. Having had substantial experience with translating survey instruments into Thai, I was familiar with the problems of making literal translations and mapping concepts from one language into another. Having had this experience, however, did not mean that I successfully avoided problems in this task of translation. Members of the Wat Lao committee then translated the English-Thai questions into Lao and typed them on their Lao typewriter at the temple. During this process, questions were added, dropped and rephrased in the process of negotiating with the resident monk for the correct phrasing. Finally, the monk typed a special prayer at the bottom of the instrument, blessing those who persevered to the bottom of the second page. The survey form included the Lao and the English sets of questions stapled together, and respondents could answer in either language.

Ambiguities remained in the questions, and in many cases, questions were probably misunderstood. The respondents were told that they did not need to answer any question they did not want to answer. Thus, substantial "missing values" also became useful information, as many Lao consistently avoided answering some question, such as the length of time spent in refugee camps in Thailand.

My husband and I offered assistance with filling out the survey forms when we were asked. Before and after the service, Lao families filled out the two-page survey; often children helped their parents. Men who were sitting together often discussed the questions with the better educated, and those more familiar with filling out forms, helping those less familiar with the process. Although there were more women than men at the service, more men returned the survey. Many older women folded the form and wrapped it up with their religious papers and paraphernalia. I saw the papers reappear at later services, not as surveys to be answered but as folded icons of sacred words appropriate to bring to temple services.

On October 18, 150 survey instruments were distributed; 111 instruments were returned with enough information to be considered for analysis. At least 10 forms were taken by Wat Lao officials to Wat Lao and were not returned. Most survey forms were completed in Lao; 16 respondents filled in the English form or a combination of the Lao and English forms. The English surveys were filled in by teenagers who could not read Lao script.

Although the survey concentrated on Buddhist practice, the characteristics of the respondents give a picture of one group of Lao refugees. Again, it is not representative of the Lao in Toronto but of the Lao who regularly attend Buddhist services. Some generalizations are possible, however, because throughout the research I sought out those who knew about or wrote about the efforts of the Lao in other cities and countries to reestablish their religious traditions. Where appropriate, these experiences are included for comparison.

# Chapter Two

## Creating the Refugee Flow

### Escape to Thailand

When the Mekong River became a national boundary between Laos and Thailand, it separated two groups of Lao. Even before the flood of Lao refugees into Thailand in the late 1970s, there were about five times more Lao on the Thai side of the Mekong River than on the Lao side. The Lao in northeastern Thailand are impoverished but independent in spirit, resisting whenever possible Bangkok's efforts to strengthen centralized control over the northeast. Thus, the flood of Lao refugees into northeastern Thailand created a dilemma for the Thai beyond the difficulties of establishing emergency relief operations. For there was real concern that individual Lao could escape from refugee camps and settle in Lao villages in northeastern Thailand, straining already meager resources in the region.

Countries of first asylum for Indochinese refugees include Thailand, Malaysia, Indonesia, the Philippines and Hong Kong. Almost all lowland Lao who left Laos as refugees entered Thailand as the country of first asylum for Indochinese refugees.

The Lao left their country for the same reasons that most refugees leave—fear for their personal safety in the form of re-education "seminars" from which they would never return; fear of unjust accusations; and their inability to meet basic subsistence needs under the new economic system. They did not leave because of religious persecution per se.

Although some Lao fled across the Mekong River in the spring of 1975, the refugee flood peaked in 1978, after the previous year's drought, and between 1975 and 1980 an estimated 400,000 people left a country of 3,500,000. Over 200,000 lowland Lao and over 120,000 upland Lao arrived in Thailand between 1975 and 1986, where they were detained as illegal immigrants and housed in detention centers. Events in Laos accounted for the pace of refugee flows into Thailand—the droughts of 1977, the efforts to collectivize farms in 1978, worsening economic conditions in 1984 and 1985. New tax regulations and military conscription laws encouraged a new wave of refugees to cross the Mekong into Thailand.

11

**Table 2.1  Resettlment of Indochinese Refugees in Countries of First Asylum**

| Country | Number of Refugees |
|---------|--------------------|
| Thailand | 125,859 |
| Philippines | 18,947 |
| Hong Kong | 12,806 |
| Malaysia | 9,823 |
| Indonesia | 7,414 |
| Japan | 1,682 |
| Macao | 770 |

Source: Chan and Loveridge 1985:747 from United Nations High Commissioner for Refugees (UNHCR) statistics of 1984.

The decision to leave Laos must not have been made easily. Plans to escape had to be made in absolute secrecy and involved amassing all possible financial resources, usually in the form of gold, before undertaking the trip across the river. One Toronto Lao said that if you knew the Thai officer at the border, you would pay about $50 per person to enter the camp, but if you did not know him, it would cost at least $250. Other research documents the amount of money needed to speed up the processing of documents ($150–250, Samart 1992). In a personal account, another Lao man described how he swam the Mekong River and then arranged to bring his family across:

> I hired a man in the camp to bring my wife and children across for $400. He walked ten kilometers through the forest on the Lao side to get my wife. Then he gave the kids sleeping pills to keep them quiet, carried them back through the forest to the river where they boarded a boat for the Thai side. I got the money for him through a Thai bank near the camp. It came from my brother in Hawaii and my brother and sister-in-law in France. (Kuamtou 1981:158)

Although I focus here on the lowland Lao, it is important to remember that in the first wave of refugees from Laos in 1975, 10,000 lowland Lao were swamped numerically by nearly 45,000 upland refugees from Laos. Currently (1992) there are in Thailand approximately 6,500 lowland Lao in holding centers and about 47,500 upland peoples from Laos; the latter have proved much more difficult to resettle, by many accounts. Over 174,000 lowland Lao have resettled in third countries, most (over 115,000) in the United States.

**Camp Experiences**

Most lowland Lao refugees are housed in Ban Napho detention center in Nakhon Phanom province, northeastern Thailand. Most of the upland groups are located in camps to the north: Chieng Kham and Ban Vinai. Ban Napho housed 17,627 Lao refugees as of June 30, 1988. Opened in 1977, Ban Napho has gradually expanded to hold nearly all the lowland Lao refugees in Thailand. The camp suffers from problems of overcrowding made more serious by the outbreak of a fire in February 1986. Both relief workers and refugees describe the rising crime rate, attributed in large part to the high percentage of bored, unoccupied single men aged fifteen to twenty-five who could not work outside the camp (2,500 total as of the end of February, 1986, CCSDPT 1986:7). The population profile in the camps indicates that about 75 percent of the refugees are between the ages of one and twenty-nine (Pongsapit and Chongwattana 1988:27). These conditions are understandable when we consider the rapid growth of the camp. In 1977 the camp contained 500 refugees; in 1980, 15,000 refugees; and in 1986, over 23,000 refugees. Water shortages and sanitation problems plagued the camp and stressed the already minimal health care facilities available in Ban Napho.

Ban Napho was a "humane deterrent" camp, with deliberately austere and basic conditions to discourage the influx of additional Lao refugees, until 1986 when resettlement was permitted for all residents in the camp. Service programs are still kept to a minimum except for basic medical care and supplemental feeding. The camp has developed a center for traditional medicine with the assistance of Dr. J. P. Hiegel, who supported the development of traditional Khmer medical centers in other camps. In a survey on refugee satisfaction with conditions in refugee camps, refugees reported over-whelming satisfaction with their present camp, regardless of conditions. This is, of course, not surprising, considering the conditions most have left in their home country. In six camps in Thailand, 85.1 percent to 98.0 percent of respondents were satisfied with their present camp. But the lowest percentage of refugees answering "yes" to the question of satisfaction came from Ban Napho, the lowland Lao camp. They were very clear about what they needed to improve the camp—more food (23.8 percent) and training and educational facilities (16.3 percent). Although a voluntary agency offered some vocational training, formal educational programs were handled by the refugees themselves with assistance from the United Nations High Commissioner for Refugees (UNHCR).

In spite of official restrictions, there was substantial trading in food, clothing and other resources within the camp, and some refugees had positions with international agencies. Other refugees were even able to leave the camp to work in neighboring rice fields or factories (Samart 1992).

Since 1985, the numbers of arrivals of lowland Lao into Thailand have become more difficult to record accurately, because the Thai government established new screening procedures for lowland Lao and the upland peoples. The screening is intended to separate out economic migrants from true refugees and return the former to Laos. The new screening procedures have led to a significant decrease in refugee arrivals from Laos. For example, between July 1985 and February 1986, 2,569 arrivals from Laos were screened, with 1,343 accepted as refugees and 783 rejected as economic migrants. Those rejected have been confined in detention camps for eventual return to Laos (CCSDPT 1986:7). In the first twelve months of the new screening, 1,100 Lao were identified as economic migrants rather than true refugees (Nakavachara and Rogge 1987:279).

The "screened out" Lao have joined a number of other Lao who are preparing for repatriation to Laos. But only 44 Lao identified as economic migrants were repatriated to Laos as of July 1988. Generally Laos has only accepted back voluntarily repatriated Lao, not those screened out as ineligible for refugee protection.

**Table 2.2 Lowland Lao Refugees and Asylum Seekers in Thailand**

| Date of Arrival | Number of Lowland Lao | Camp Situations |
|---|---|---|
| 1975 | 10,195 | Ubon camp opens |
| 1976 | 19,499 | Nong Khai camp opens |
| 1977 | 18,070 | Ban Napho camp opens |
| 1978 | 48,781 | |
| 1979 | 22,045 | Ubon camp holds 79,000 |
| 1980 | 28,967 | Ban Napho camp holds 15,000 |
| | | Nong Khai camp holds 30,000 |
| | | Ubon camp holds 28,820 |
| 1981 | 16,377 | Ban Napho camp expanded |
| 1982 | 3,203 | Ubon camp holds 9,867 |
| | | Ban Napho holds 12,186 |
| 1983 | 4,571 | Ubon closes except for Lao to be repatriated |
| | | All Lao housed at Ban Napho |
| 1984 | 14,616 | Ban Napho holds 20,000 |
| 1985 | 13,344 | Ban Napho holds 42,000 (peak) |
| 1986 | 2,911 | Ban Napho holds 23,465 |
| 1987 | 0 | |
| 1988 | 0 | Ban Napho holds 17,627 (June 30, 1988) |
| 1989 | 0 | Ban Napho holds 14,720 (June 30, 1989) |

Source: UNHCR, Bangkok

   Durable solutions for Lao refugees include resettlement in third countries, local resettlement in Thailand and voluntary repatriation. The third option, voluntary repatriation, is more possible for the Lao than for any other group of Southeast Asian refugees. The Lao government agreed to voluntary repatriation in 1980. However, up to the end of 1988 only 2,406 Lao refugees had returned under this program organized by UNHCR and the Thai government. In 1988, the reduced opportunities for resettlement, greater openness and development in Laos and improved relations between Thailand and Laos resulted in an increasing amount of voluntary repatriation. The current Thai policy is to encourage all lowland Lao to repatriate. However, since the screening for asylum seekers began in 1985, there has been potential for confusing voluntary repatriation cases and economic migrants, although officially no distinction is made on the Lao side. UNHCR counselors in the Thai camps advise the Lao who wish to repatriate concerning their options and help them fill out applications, which are then sent on to Lao government authorities.

**Table 2.3 Voluntary Repatriation of Lowland Lao Refugees**

| Date | Number of Refugees |
|------|--------------------|
| 1981 | 279 |
| 1982 | 791 |
| 1983 | 515 |
| 1984 | 200 |
| 1985 | 101 |
| 1986 | 134 |
| 1987 | 33 |
| 1988 | 160 |
| 1989 | 1,424 |
| 1990 | 529 |
| <u>1991</u> | <u>539</u> |
| Total | 4,898 |

<u>Source:</u> UNHCR, Bangkok

Refugees must sign a declaration that they are repatriating voluntarily. UNHCR provides all returnees with a package of 2,000 baht, 28,000 kip (about $150 Cdn. total) and 18 months' supply of rice per person. Those who have chosen to repatriate in a group settlement also receive a small plot of farming land, a house plot, and tools for house construction. Various (NGOs) nongovernmental organizations may provide refugees with essential items such as clothes, shoes, medicine, hand tools, dried foods, mosquito nets, blankets, floor mats, buckets and kitchen utensils. By March 1992, about 5,000 lowland Lao had been repatriated under UNHCR auspices, but 18,000 are estimated to have repatriated independently (spontaneous repatriation).

There has been little follow-up of repatriated Lao in their local communities, although a study of Lao repatriation is now being undertaken by the Institute of Asian Studies, Chulalongkorn University, Bangkok. Clearly, if repatriation is to be expanded as a solution for Lao refugees currently in Thai camps, it must be accompanied by more attention to local development projects designed to rebuild the economic base of a country devastated by war. UNHCR has considered this by providing schools, health care, irrigation projects and vocational training to areas of Laos that receive significant numbers of repatriated Lao. Since 1980, twenty-five such projects have been funded, costing $3,800,000 (Rabé 1990:27).

Pongsapit and Chongwatana argue that conditions in Laos and the reorientation program of the Lao government discourage repatriation. The process may take up to four months, and returnees often cannot be returned to their village of origin.

The Lao government has agreed to increase the maximum number of places for returnees from 150 to 300 per month and to register returnees as full citizens. This streamlined procedure allows Lao refugees to move from camps back to their homes within a few weeks (Jambor 1990:32). This also reduces the opportunities for corruption. Because lowland Lao have not been part of the forced returns (unlike Khmer and Hmong refugees), repatriation appears to be a serious policy option for the lowland Lao, more than for the Khmer or Vietnamese. But the process is slow, and agencies are careful to observe the principle of *non-refoulement* (no return of refugees to conditions of danger). More significantly, agencies must ensure against using misleading information regarding conditions in Laos. Although the Hmong in Ban Vinai camp knew very little about conditions in Laos or the repatriation program, they considered the UNHCR "naive" for believing it could adequately protect returnees in Laos (Rabé 1990:31).

Life in refugee camps is characterized by waiting—for documents, for interviews, for information—and when the waiting is done for the moment, there are lines to form to wait again for more tangible objectives such as a stamp, a health check, a food donation. But there is a superficial sense of purpose about the available activities: carrying documents from one part of camp to the other, visiting the health center, chatting with friends, playing volleyball, sitting in classes for language or Bible study, selling fresh vegetables or cold pop, learning to fit prostheses, hustling for opportunities to be interviewed for resettlement. When the hustling stops, the suicides begin, for the refugee has given up hope, and even the thought of responsibility to family members is not a sufficient hold on a life without promise of improvement in present conditions or reduction of uncertainties. The apparent purposelessness of any action combined with the incredible boredom of camp life produces in some refugees a crisis of despair resulting in suicide. Even in death, these refugees continue to affect their camp communities, as word quickly spreads about the hanging or the drug overdose, fueling talk of mass suicide. One suicide of a Vietnamese man in a Thai camp further escalated fears when his friend, possessed by the spirit of the suicide victim, urged others to commit suicide too. I return to these mental health issues in the last chapter.

Conditions are particularly difficult for women who become victims of violence, rape and forced marriages, as men react to the overcrowding and boredom of camp life by abusing women. One afternoon, in my dining room, a Lao teenager compared notes with several Lao men about how many women they had raped during their camp stay. Although this is only an anecdote from an overheard conversation, it fits with other reports on life in the Lao camps. Women without family support are often forced into prostitution after such sexual assaults.

Lowland Lao in the refugee camps in Thailand may have been in the camps anywhere from a few months to more than ten years. Children are born and grow up in the camps without ever having lived in the country their parents left. The survey of Lao Buddhists in Toronto revealed that the Lao refugees had spent from a few months to eight years in refugee camps in Thailand.

**Table 2.4 Time Spent in Refugee Camps**

| Time Spent | Percentage | Number Respondents |
|---|---|---|
| Less than one year | 37.2 | 35 |
| One to two years | 31.9 | 30 |
| Two to three years | 19.1 | 19 |
| Three to four years | 3.2 | 3 |
| Six to seven years | 1.1 | 1 |
| Seven to nine years | 1.1 | 1 |
| Never resided in a camp | 6.4 | 6 |

Seventeen refugees of the 111 answering the survey did not indicate how long they had been in the camps. Possibly they truly do not know, for to them time may have stopped as they crossed the Mekong and started again in the country of final asylum. Others responded by specifying the number of years, months, days and hours spent in the camps.

Camp life is not totally isolated for the lowland Lao. They receive both mail and money from overseas. Their relatives send whatever they can spare, and these small amounts keep economic activities going in the camps. The Lao receive more money from their relatives overseas (about $600 annually) than other ethnic groups in refugee camps in Thailand (Pongsapit and Chongwattana 1988:46). Lao relatives in Toronto, for example, regularly send money back to their relatives in camps, keeping alive the connections that make resettlement possible. Money is needed to maintain families in the camps and to arrange for additional family members to enter refugee camps in Thailand. In Thai refugee camps such as Ban Napho and Panat Nikhom, evidence for some of the overseas donations from relatives and friends in Australia and Canada is proudly displayed on the walls of makeshift temples. On the cement walls of a building used as a Buddhist center at Panat Nikhom are life size paintings depicting the Buddha's life, with the amount of donations from Lao families in Canada neatly enumerated in the corners.

### Religion in the Camps

> One of the major causes of emotional distress and psychological breakdown among refugees is the extent to which the fragmentation and dislocations which have taken place in their external lives are mirrored by a corresponding shattering of internal reality. The refugee loses track not only of where he has come from and the traumas that have befallen him, but also of who he was and therefore, also, of who he now is. (Chan and Loveridge 1987:756)

The loss of a meaningful sense of identity is complicated by the emphasis in camps and orientation programs on preparation for the future—putting the pain of the past behind. However, the lack of opportunities to reconstruct and reassemble parts of the past separates refugees from the cultural resources they need for building new personal and social strategies for successful adaptation. One of the most important cultural resource for guiding both individual and community action among the Lao and Khmer is Theravada Buddhism. But life in the camps makes it difficult to call on the spiritual resource of Theravada Buddhism. And where Buddhist resources are scarcest, Christian resources abound.

Since most of the NGOs working in the refugee camps are religious--mostly Christian—it is not surprising that there are a variety of opportunities for expanding knowledge about Christianity and ultimately expanding the flock. Most informants suggested that overall, the pressures to convert to Christianity are subtle but insidious. Pressures to attend services or study groups or convert build from the refugees perceived obligation to the NGO personnel and their gratitude for the help within the camps. Recommendations for relieving the mental health crisis in the Thai-Khmer border camps include strictly enforcing the UN prohibitions against religious proselytizing in the camps (Mollica 1990:144).

The Committee for the Coordination of Services to Displaced Persons in Thailand (CCSDPT) identified forty member groups working in Thai refugee camps in 1988. (Since 1986, two voluntary groups have left the CCSDPT, and one new one has joined.) These include international organizations such as the United Nations High Commissioner for Refugees (UNHCR) and the International Red Cross, along with a number of voluntary agencies. Of these, twenty-one have Christian affiliation and one is Zen Buddhist. The Christian groups vary from groups like the Young Women's Christian Association (YWCA) whose activities are not primarily religious to groups like Youth With a Mission (YWAM) whose activities are strongly evangelical and geared toward conversion. These groups provide important medical, educational and other support services for the refugees. The service providers are not supposed to proselytize or convert. However, the dominant Christian presence is very obvious to refugees, and the Christian groups have the most extensive resources and services. There are reports of missionaries using relief supplies and promises of resettlement to induce Khmer refugees to convert in Khao I Dang camp (Gosling 1984:62) for example. Other workers describe mass baptisms in water when the camps were so short of water that no one had bathed for days.

It is difficult to estimate the number of converts from Buddhism to Christianity that have taken place in the refugee camps. In an examination of the changing religious identity of 199 Southeast Asian refugees in the United States, Burwell and coauthors noted that of the 91 refugees identifying themselves as Buddhist in the camps, only 57 still identified themselves as Buddhist at the time of an interview in the United States a few months later. The authors point out that this may be merely a shift in religious social identification and may not signify religious conversion. They write that "a Christian church may simply provide a functional alternative to a Buddhist temple but because one is attending a church the individual identifies him/herself as a Christian" (Burwell et al. 1986:360). Yet some of these refugees reverted to their Buddhist identity after a few months in North America, possibly as they discovered that alternative religious identities (including Buddhist) may be acceptable in North America (Burwell et al.1986:363).

Refugee workers and refugees suggest that there are substantial differences between Catholic and Protestant activities in the refugee camps. The majority of the NGOs with a Christian affiliation are Protestant. Since there are few Southeast Asian Protestant ministers, the majority of the service providers and missionaries in the camps are foreign.

This is not always the case in the Catholic NGO community, since a number of Vietnamese refugees were already Catholic in Vietnam, and there were Vietnamese Catholic priests in some of the camps. These Vietnamese priests are very strict but live "like kings" compared to the other refugees, according to a Vietnamese refugee converted to a Protestant denomination while in Panat Nikhom camp. In addition, the Catholic Office for Emergency Relief and Refugees (COERR), a very active group in a number of refugee camps in Thailand, are staffed with Thai Catholic priests.

Reasons for camp conversions to Christianity are not hard to understand. Refugees convert largely to "thank" the Christian relief workers and to increase their chances of resettlement. Conversion also neutralizes the problems caused by spirits; both physical and mental discomfort can be reduced once refugees are "free of spirits." In resettlement countries, spirits are unlikely to be a major concern. "They are not our spirits, we don't know them, nor do they know us. So how can they affect us and us them?" (Desan 1983:46). Other researchers make it clear that spirits are still a significant problem for Southeast Asian refugees in North America (Muecke 1987). However, the refugees will no longer have the cultural resources, including ritual practitioners, to combat them. Thus, conversion to Christianity may be considered a strategy to ensure that spirits are no longer a threat. However, informants were unwilling to discuss spirits, and the relation between conversion and spirits remains to be explored.

When refugees are at their most vulnerable, they can be easily convinced of the "failure" of Buddhism to protect them. In this line of argument lies great anguish, firing up doubts that even the most spiritually sensitive people have in the face of devastating loss. This line of argument may have been particularly effective with Cambodian refugees who faced the irrational destruction by the Pol Pot regime, including the systematic destruction of Khmer Buddhist institutions.

The most useful perspective for viewing the relation between conversion and mental health comes from the work of Dr. J. P. Hiegel, who has set up a number of traditional healing centers for Lao and Khmer in refugee camps in Thailand. His work has been opposed by Christian health workers who object to his developing indigenous health services to address the physical and mental needs of the refugees. As Christians and missionaries, they feel they are "responsible for the spiritual well-being of their patients and think it their duty to discourage them from accepting any kind of treatment involving magic" (Hiegel 1984:40). He was called a "devil stronger than Jesus" by Christian coworkers. They viewed the Southeast Asian medical system with its overlap between physical, mental, and spiritual health as a threat to western biomedical theories of comparmentalization and disease causation. In his practice, he came across a number of psychological problems caused by camp conversions. He writes:

> I have seen three Buddhist refugees who suffered a psychotic episode after being baptized; they were borderline psychotics and could not withstand the conflict of identity between the Buddhist and the Christian parts of themselves. One woman clearly projected her conflict into her hallucinations: she developed a hallucinary psychosis in which she could hear Buddha speaking to her through one ear and the "Christian God" through the other. (Hiegel 1984:41)

In another case illustrating the conflicts between Buddhist and Christian beliefs, Hiegel describes

> a young Lao presented with a very high degree of psychotic anxiety after being baptized. His self-esteem had suffered severely as he had the feeling that his religion, Buddhism, and his cultural beliefs, and consequently part of his own self, were "bad." At the same time as he maintained that he was still Buddhist, he felt much guilt because he had agreed to become Christian, which seemed to him to be a betrayal of his father and his ancestors. (Hiegel 1984:41)

The activities around conversion in the camps are difficult to interpret because there is a reluctance among both refugees and service providers to discuss them. This is fully understandable, since complex personal emotions are involved. The question of camp conversions is a particularly sensitive issue because humanitarian aid in refugee camps is so dependent on Christian NGOs and on volunteer and low paid assistance in the delivery of services. In the following quote, the pastor of a rural church in Minnesota makes the relation between sponsorship and conversion painfully clear:

> If the church hadn't planned to convert the refugees, we never would have bothered to bring this family to this particular town. We wanted to help them find Christ. . . . . If they are going to hell, they might as well go to hell from Cambodia as from Minnesota. It would be wicked to just bring them over and feed and clothe them and let them go to hell. The God who made us wants them to be converted. (Williams 1989:68)

Buddhism is not actively encouraged in the camps although there are Lao and Khmer monks. In fact, monks may have a better chance of being considered "refugees," although this may result in a number of "men in yellow robes" who are not ordained. Among the Vietnamese refugees, there are a number of Buddhist monks and temporary temples in the camps. In the summer of 1988, there were also several Buddhist nuns. The monks held informal services, taught children about Buddhism, led meditation sessions and generally helped refugees cope with the tensions and uncertainties of camp life. In Panat Nikhom camp, cremation ceremonies are allowed outside the camp at a local Buddhist temple (Benyasut 1989:54).

Although ordination in Lao and Khmer camps is possible, it is difficult because of the problem of legitimacy— both of the temple and the preceptors. The ordainands are not registered with the Thai Buddhist order (the Sangha), and as displaced persons, they can not be registered with the Lao or Khmer Sangha. Ordination requires that a candidate is not in breach of the law. Since Khmer and Lao are considered illegal aliens in Thailand, there is a question whether novices and monks can be legitimately ordained in the camps.

For the Khmer, as for the Lao, Buddhism was a main source of learning and the means of transmitting culture to the younger generation. Gyallay-Pap points out the disparity between the modern school curriculum established in the Khmer border camps and the realities of Khmer culture and society. Although there were temples at the peripheries of the camps, he was "hard pressed to find an authentic and informed Khmer Buddhist culture being transmitted through the education system to the Cambodian young in the camps" (Gyallay-Pap 1989:273). He voices concern as to whether the Khmer Buddhist Sangha, decimated by the Khmer Rouge, can renew its standards and recover its place of honor in Khmer society.

In Ban Napho, for example, 94 percent of the camp refugees are practicing Buddhists, but after the small thatch hut with a papier-mâché Buddha image burned down, the religious facilities in the camp consisted of four brick Christian churches. The refugees tried to raise money to build a temple, but no refugee support groups responded. However, a visiting Japanese trade delegation asked what the camp needed and when a Buddhist temple was suggested, they donated enough funds to build an impressive structure, which now needs an equally impressive Buddha image instead of the small one they can afford.

Canadian Lao have donated money for Buddhist activities, including painting murals of the life of the Buddha on the cement walls of camp buildings, sponsoring merit-making rituals and donating funds to purchase Buddhist texts. The Lao in Toronto donated the texts to a temple in Nong Khai, important to these Lao refugees, although it was not in the refugee camp. As will be discussed later, when there is no recognized temple within a camp, many overseas Lao who want to make merit for their deceased relatives prefer to donate to an established Thai temple—clearly a legitimate field of merit--rather than to a makeshift unauthorized temple of dubious legitimacy within the camps.

This situation may change now that there is a newly built permanent temple in Ban Napho, dedicated in July 1988. A camp official suggested that the Lao in Toronto might consider making a special donation to this new temple to purchase a suitable Buddha image for the temple. This would be a very special act of merit making. In this way, the Lao in refugee camps and the resettled Lao in Canada could see themselves connected in a single moral community, however separated geographically.

At Ban Napho in the summer of 1988, there were over sixty novices, but there were only a very few monks who had been ordained for ten years or more. Most have been monks for two or three years, and some refugees have suggested that they have simply "put on the robes" to get across the border. But there are special difficulties concerning monks as refugees. Although they are needed for the large refugee populations in resettled areas in North America, they are also needed in the camps and needed to reinvigorate the religious system on their return to their home countries. If repatriation becomes a viable option, then the monks currently in refugee camps may have the potential to play an important role in resettlement activities, particularly in Laos.

To phrase the dilemma in the crudest of terms, refugees quickly learn that in the camps and in their new homelands, Buddhism costs and Christianity pays. For some, the costs of reestablishing and maintaining Buddhism are simply too high. As a result, at the time when their spiritual needs may be greatest, they opt for "doing nothing" about religion, the option for about 50 percent to 60 percent of the Hmong in the Philadelphia area (Desan 1983:45).

**Entering Canada**

The United States has received about half the lowland Lao who have escaped from Laos (102,783), followed by France (25,070), Canada (12,793), Australia (7,034) and China (2,503) (UNHCR, 1986). Canada often had been the second or third choice for resettlement. In 1978, Indochinese refugees became one of three designated classes of admissible refugees to Canada (Neuwirth and Rogge 1988:251). Before the largest intake of Lao refugees in 1979 and 1980, there were almost no Lao immigrants to Canada except for a very few students. Thus, there were no Lao immigrant groups to assist with the resettlement of the Lao refugees in Canada. According to Canadian Employment and Immigration Commission (CEIC) statistics, 11 Lao refugees entered Canada in 1975 and 6,264 in 1980.

The greatest concentration of Southeast Asian refugees into Canada occurred after 1978. Between 1975 and 1984, about 85,000 individuals arrived from Vietnam, Kampuchea and Laos as refugees and designated class immigrants; more recent refugee arrivals and immigrants brought the total to 120,000 refugees from Southeast Asia since 1978 (Indra 1988:155). Of these, about 16,000 have been lowland Lao.

Lao refugees have entered Canada as both government-sponsored and private sponsored refugees. Government-sponsored refugees are funded through the CEIC and the Secretary of State. Private sponsors provide financial and moral support to refugees for one year after arrival. Under private sponsorship, five or more Canadians contract with the federal government to provide these services. Although private sponsorship was expected to be much more effective than government sponsorship, Indra (1988) found a number of structural constraints that have reduced this potential. I reviewed some of the problems emerging out of in-house sponsorship, where refugees live with their sponsors. Many conflicts have developed from different conceptions of sponsorship, reciprocity and sharing (P. Van Esterik 1981).

Private sponsorship involves substantial participation by religious institutions and organizations. In fact, grass-roots humanitarian concerns have been disseminated through churches, to a large extent. Sixty-five percent of the 6,887 sponsorship groups created between January 1, 1979, and December 31, 1980, operated through religious organizations. The Mennonite Central Committee, Christian Reformed Church, Roman Catholic Church and the United Church, played particularly active roles; almost half of all privately sponsored refugees have been supported by church groups (Indra 1988:156). Groups such as the Christian Reformed Congregations have supported refugees because "as Christians, they wish to express their sense of spiritual gratitude through concrete good works" (Adelman 1982:114).

Sponsorship by church organizations has extended beyond the provision of basic services to attempts to integrate refugees into church communities. Indra writes:

> This typically involved bringing them to church services and other church events, visiting other church members in their homes, and introducing refugees to other refugees sponsored by other members of the same congregations. Many attempted the conversion of refugees sponsored by members of their congregations. (Indra 1988:159)

Beiser hypothesizes that "psychological conflict engendered by the difference between church-based sponsor's religion and Southeast Asian ones countered any positive effects arising from the closer personal relations engendered by private sponsorship" (Beiser 1988b:77). Indeed, pressures to have refugees attend the sponsors' church may have led to many conflicts. A Vietnamese refugee who was privately sponsored stated his feeling clearly: "I lived with them for a month when I first came and had a hard time dealing with them. I refused to go to church with them" (Woon 1987:136).

## Lao in Toronto

The common perception of both Lao and those who work with refugees is that the best-educated Lao settled in Quebec. Since their higher education was in French, they preferred to resettle in a Francophone area, leaving the less-educated rural villagers to settle elsewhere in the country. Thus, Quebec Lao are perceived to be "doing better" than those in Ontario. However, in spite of their French-language training there is substantial secondary migration to Ontario for work. Older adults prefer to be on Quebec welfare, where they do not have to seek employment beyond the age of fifty-five. The elders are then free to spend more time at the Lao temples. According to the 1986 census, about 28 percent of Lao in Canada live in Quebec and about 40 percent in Ontario (Samart 1992:61).

The lowland Lao in Toronto number approximately 7,000. The exact number is difficult to calculate because of the constant secondary migration from other provinces. Not all Lao register with the Lao Association of Ontario (LAO) nor maintain contact with other Lao groups. Recent arrivals of Lao refugees from Thai camps are few in number and seldom government sponsored. For example, there were no government-sponsored Lao refugees arriving in Toronto in 1985. Private sponsorship is most often accomplished through small groups of Lao bringing family members or close friends from the camps. Family sponsorship is particularly difficult because sponsoring relatives are hardly able to assist their relatives with English classes and job training since they are still struggling themselves. The process of sponsoring new family members is long and slow, but there are enough brokers in the community and in associations such as LAO to assist with the paper work. Among the Lao survey respondents, 40.2 percent were government-sponsored refugees, 38.3 percent were sponsored by a church group, 15.9 percent by Lao relatives (private sponsorship) and 5.6 percent by a private non-Lao sponsorship group.

On arrival in Toronto, the Lao prefer to settle in the downtown area close to government services if they do not have families to assist them. Over time, families move north into subsidized apartments in the city's suburbs. The Lao tend to cluster in a number of areas in Toronto, with about half living quite close to the Lao Association, the apartment serving as the Lao temple and several industrial complexes. The new homeowners have moved farther north to the more distant suburbs.

The following tables refer to the Lao survey respondents and provide a basic description of that group. In spite of the fact that more women attended the service on October 18, 54.1 percent of the respondents were male and 45.9 percent female (missing values, 2). Their ages ranged from fourteen to seventy years of age.

## Table 2.5 Age of Respondents

| Age Group | Percent of Respondents |
|---|---|
| 20 and below | 2.1 |
| 21 to 30 | 19.7 |
| 31 to 40 | 31.8 |
| 41 to 50 | 9.6 |
| 51 to 60 | 7.5 |
| Over 60 | 9.3 |

Those who took the survey form and did not return it were mainly elderly women. Although the elderly lead the chants and know the sermons and services most accurately, there are a good number of younger adults at the services too. Teenagers and children are present at many services but, as will be discussed later, they say that they do not know what is going on. Their responses to questions about religion clearly demonstrate this lack of understanding.

At the time of the survey, 9 percent of the respondents were unemployed, 10.1 percent were students and 10.1 percent were women who worked in the house. The Lao phrasing of the question translates almost exactly as "staying in the house." The majority of the Lao, both men and women, work as laborers (27 percent) or at semiskilled jobs (14.6 percent) such as furniture maker, forklift operator, sewing machine operator and dressmaker. Many Lao are concentrated in semiskilled factory work in the manufacture of car parts and furniture (Gordon 1990:18).

A very few have higher-paying positions as office or government workers (6.7 percent), as mechanics or welders (7.9 percent) or in health-related jobs (4.5 percent). However, twenty-two respondents made no attempt to indicate in Lao or English what they did. From informal conversations, it is clear that Lao women in particular pick up a wide range of jobs in factories, many of which are "unofficial." That is, women describe going in with their friends and being "allowed" to work overtime or at night to make extra money because their supervisors "like Lao people." There is an excellent possibility that many Lao women in particular are exploited, since they are not familiar with their rights as workers. However, they are very anxious not to identify their employers because they consider their informal work opportunities as special favors from patrons and not as exploitative behavior.

The Lao education system consists of primary school (*pathom*), middle school (*mathayom*), high school (*udom*) and post-secondary school (*mahavitayalay*). The first four years of mandatory schooling are presumed to provide general literacy, but for peasant families in Laos, even a primary education might not provide true literacy if there is no opportunity to read following the primary grades. Table 2.6 shows the respondents' education in Laos.

**Table 2.6 Education of Respondents in Laos**

| Educational Level | Percent of Respondents |
|-------------------|------------------------|
| No education | 16.5 |
| Primary school | 25.8 |
| Middle school | 12.4 |
| High school | 38.1 |
| Post secondary | 7.2 |

It is likely that many claimed a high school education even if they did not complete or pass the year. However, the data provide a general indication of the educational background of the Lao refugees attending the Buddhist service. Pongsapit and Chongwattana record the educational attainment of lowland Lao in refugee camps in Thailand in 1987.(Table 2.7) These figures also demonstrate the low educational attainment of lowland Lao refugees generally.

**Table 2.7 Educational Attainment of Lao refugees in Thai Camps**

| Educational Level | Percent of Refugees |
|---|---|
| No education | 45.40 |
| Primary school | 36.52 |
| Mid/high school | 14.81 |
| Post secondary* | 1.45 |

Source: Pongsapit and Chongwattana 1988:27
*Vocational plus university graduate

After arriving in Canada, most Lao (54.3 percent) did not continue their formal education. However, a good number returned to school for some education at the high school level (29.3 percent) and post-secondary level (4.3 percent). This was probably only a realistic option for younger Lao who had not been away from school for too many years. For older Lao, even the English as a Second Language (ESL) classes taken by 69.4 percent of the respondents were a strain. However, over 80 percent of the respondents claimed that they spoke and understood English. In conversation, most of the Lao women preferred to respond to my conversational Thai with Lao, even considering the differences between these two related languages. They seldom initiated a conversation in English other than a brief greeting. A number of adult men were fluent in English, but except for Lao Association leaders who were used to conversing in English, they too preferred to chat in a combination of Thai and Lao.

The respondents lived in Canada an average of eight and a half years, which would place their arrival around 1979, the period of heaviest refugee intake. Two respondents had been here less than a year and one had been in Canada for nineteen years, the only Lao immigrant to have arrived in Canada before 1975.

In this chapter, I have examined the historical context of Lao refugees, including the creation of the refugee flow, their escape to Thailand, life in the Thai camps and resettlement in Canada. The survey respondents provide a snapshot of a particular group of Lao refugees—a group that is the focus of the following chapters. The next chapter explores Buddhism and the refugee experience in more detail, as a background for understanding the establishment of Lao Buddhism in North America.

# Chapter Three

## Buddhism and the Refugee Experience

### Refugees and Religion

*"While trends in social and economic orientation have been recorded, no similar surveys have focused on the religious adaptation of the newcomers. The subject is a difficult one to reduce to numbers or graphs: it concerns the spiritual readjustment of a people" (Desan 1983:45). "Most research on refugee resettlement has focused upon economic factors such as employment, housing and family assistance" (Burwell et al. 1986:356). A review of the role of religious affiliations in refugee settlement (Winland 1992) supports these statements by North American researchers and emphasizes how little work has been done on refugees and religion in North America.*

For an annotated bibliography on the resettlement of Indochinese refugees in the United States, Ashmun located 25 references to religion in 1,037 entries. Of these, 16 referred to the religious background of the refugees in guidebooks for sponsors or service providers, 4 used religion as a variable to define refugee populations or measure acculturation, 2 referred to the existence of mutual assistance associations (MAAs) or religious organizations and 1 referred to North American religious practices. Only 2 references (out of 1,037) dealt with religion itself as a means of understanding the refugee experience. When religion is mentioned, the observations made are of little analytical value: for example, "Some Southeast Asians may attend a local Buddhist Church" (Copeland 1988:108).

In her exhaustive survey and bibliography on social science research on Southeast Asian refugees in Canada, Indra reviews work on psychological and physical health needs, family problems and social service needs and notes that "research on the rise of religious institutions, cultural celebrations or community level attempts at cultural maintenance has remained quite sparse" (Indra 1987:11). In addition, most research has been on Vietnamese, with little comparable work on Lao or Khmer. In Indra's words, the Lao and Khmer "have been systematically ignored" (Indra 1987:12). It is thus not surprising that Theravada Buddhism,

33

the tradition followed by the Lao and Khmer, is largely unknown or misunderstood in North America, except among western meditators.

A few themes emerge from refugee materials that mention religion. A minor theme concerns the theological justification for assisting refugees, particularly by Christian groups such as Church World Service. Occasionally, religion is used to "explain" some aspects of Lao behavior in North America. For example, Zaharlick and Brainard (1988) argue that since Buddhism does not stand in the way of family planning, Lao women in North America may experience a rapid fertility decline once they have access to contraception. But these are not studies of religion per se, nor do they build on indigenous religious concepts.

Other themes emerging from the few available studies include the argument that religious differences lead to conflicts among refugees. Carlin and Sokoloff (1985:97) argue that there are many religions in Southeast Asia and that some are incompatible with western cultural values, creating conflicts in worldviews. On the contrary, it seems more likely that most conflicts appear to center on conversion to Christianity or nonadherence to any religious tradition. In a study of mental health issues affecting immigrants and refugees in Canada, Beiser cites the story of a three-year-old Vietnamese girl asking her Buddhist mother about Jesus. The lesson from this incident has little to do with religiosity:

> The girl will quickly learn that she can never divest herself of her Buddhist mother. . . . The realization that they can never become what they are being taught is the best thing to be breeds frustration, which may lead to symptoms of emotional disorder or to antisocial behavior later in life." (Beiser 1988b:69)

Religion was a variable in Chan and Lam's study of Sino-Vietnamese refugees in Montreal. Among twenty-five informants, there were two Christians and twenty-three who combined ancestor worship with Buddhism (Chan and Lam 1987b:29). Yet despite intensive exploration of personal loss and bereavement, religion was not referred to by respondents or analysts as being relevant to the discussion of psychological adjustment.

It is this linkage between religion and mental health that we would expect to find developed in the literature. On the one hand, practitioners stress the importance of religion in mental health programs (cf. Bliatout et al. 1985; Owen 1985; Rumbaut 1985). An immigrant women's support group, in a deposition on mental health issues, argued that religious institutions "reinforce personal faith which can act as a buffer to stress" (Beiser 1988b). In a workshop on the psychological needs of long-term refugees, one speaker identified the need to "continue to utilize the spiritual resources that were helpful in providing strength in the past" (Johnston 1988:3:2).

It is therefore difficult to understand why religion and religious institutions are not considered in research or programs on mental health. For example, Beiser's recent report (1988b) subtitled *Mental Health Issues Affecting Immigrants and Refugees in Canada*, makes almost no mention of religion in its analysis. In the accompanying review of the literature on migrant mental health, religion is not considered as a variable related to risk of mental disorders. The report concludes that "the most effective measures for preventing mental ill health address the issues of socioeconomic status and socio-cultural support" (Beiser 1988b). Although the reports clearly recognize that remedial mental health services are underutilized by the refugee community, the recommendations for action center on changes to mental health programs rather than encouraging support for religious institutions (Beiser 1988b:ii). Religious institutions provide the only relevant mental health support for many Southeast Asian refugees, but those resources are seldom integrated into mental health programs in North America.

Those most familiar with Southeast Asian refugee communities in North America are aware of the complex role Buddhist monks play as service providers—usually untrained—for a wide variety of refugee problems, including mental health problems. Owen notes that "for the Khmer, the Buddhist church is increasingly becoming the focal point for seeking community support and spiritual strength, and for fostering mutual help/self-help activities" (Owen 1985:157). Often religion is not explicitly mentioned, although researchers are aware that programs should build on the resourcefulness, supportiveness and efficacy of the Indochinese community to build morale and cohesion (Chan 1987:129). In Lao and

Khmer communities, morale and cohesion is most evident in Buddhist associations and Buddhist practice. Often, this is the only place where consensus and trust can exist in factionalized communities.

Religious change and conversion has been of interest to a few researchers. Lewis and coauthors examined religiosity among Indochinese refugees in Utah and found that people changed religion for interpersonal considerations and to establish certain support networks.(Lewis et al. 1988). Burwell and coauthors (1986) explored how religion relates to the process of resettlement and developed a means of predicting changes in religious identity. (Burwell et al.1986) Both these studies will be discussed later with regard to conversion. However, it is clear that analysis of survey data reveals little about religiosity or content of beliefs. Many Indochinese Buddhists have stated that they are Buddhists even if they go to a Christian church.

Few authors give any indication of the meaning of Buddhism to refugees. The following excerpts suggest the power Buddhist beliefs have for refugee women. The first quote is from a Lao woman from Vientiane living in Bowling Green, Kentucky:

> When I was old enough to sit, I listened with Mother to the monks' teaching at the *wat* (temple) after *tak bat* (offering food to monks). The (monk) taught me how to pay respect not only to the Buddha, but also to the monks and older people, especially my parents. You show the same kind of reverence to parents and teachers as toward the Buddha. Mother and I did not stay long at the *wat* (temple)—only old people have time to stay all day and listen—but when we left we felt we had gained a certain peace of mind, as well as an understanding of how we should act in life. The more I listened, the better I felt. It made me feel proud in a way and I valued this very highly. (Burford 1981:53)

The second quote is from a Khmer widow living in San Diego County, California:

> If I have any time left from this, I would just dedicate it to worshipping the Lord Buddha and promoting

Buddhism in our community. I think that's all I can
and must do. . . . Buddhism helps me accept my fate
more easily. Buddhist teaching taught us to do good
deeds which later will be returned to us by someone
else. So whatever has happened to me so far is a
reflection of a deed that I had done in the past.
(Rumbaut 1985:475)

For the latter woman in particular, the pain of becoming a
refugee only makes sense through Buddhism.

Some of the explanations for this lack of interest in and
support for religious institutions at the official level may be
sought in government regulations. For example, in Canada,
multicultural grants from the secretary of state are made to
ethnic organizations. Indra reviews how the Secretary of State
funding requirements affected the origin and structure of
Indochinese community organizations (Indra 1987:154).
Separation of church and state principles prohibit the direct
funding of religious groups or institutions. Khamchong
Luangpraseut, supervisor of the Indochinese programs in the
Santa Ana School District in California, identifies two
additional reasons for this obvious gap in the literature:

The spiritual needs of refugees are a low priority in
most resettlement policies. . . this is a post industrialist
society which places constant emphasis on materialistic
wealth as an acceptable if not unique measure of
success in life. (Luangpraseut 1989:7)

On the other hand, among Lao communities, and possibly
Khmer as well, Buddhism is the clearest commonality and
basis for agreement within the community. Within Lao
Buddhist associations, factional and regional differences are
minimized.

Similar bureaucratic constraints existed in France.
Lanphier notes the lack of visibility or influence of cultural
organizations for Indochinese refugees in France, since before
1981, "no organization could receive a federal charter or
official recognition unless it was composed of a majority of
French nationals, who exclusively constituted its executive
echelon" (Lanphier 1987:304). However, Condominas and
others have documented the importance of the Lao Buddhist
temples in France and the thriving Buddhist community there

(Condominas 1987). Condominas refers to three temples around Paris with the prospect of several more. But forming the Lao Buddhist associations to support the temples was made difficult by a French law requiring payment of subscription for membership. "The monks and the head of the association, a Catholic Lao familiar with the intricacies of French law, found a solution allowing people to make a gift to the *Sangha* and thereby to acquire merit, rather than to pay a subscription" (Condominas 1987:450).

With so little research available on refugees and religion it is difficult to make any generalizations about the process of religious adaptation in Canada. Trends are not obvious yet, and the process is too poorly understood to risk premature analysis. So much depends on the family background, the experiences during flight and the receiving community that it is inappropriate to separate certain patterns as being typically Lao or Vietnamese. However, there are models available that may guide future analysis on this topic.

Dorais's discussion of Nguyên Huy's model of sociolinguistic adaptation of Vietnamese refugees identifies three periods: installation, lasting from the first to the third year; integration, lasting from about the third to the sixth year; and (for some refugees) identification, after this period. Non integrating refugees stress their religious traditions, ancestor worship, Buddhism and conservative Catholicism. In the third period of identification, most refugees still participate in community celebrations like Têt, the lunar New Year. A smaller group of Vietnamese refugees have their Vietnamese identity reinforced after a period of successful integration (Dorais 1987:61–62).

This possibility of reverting to a strong Vietnamese identity underscores the necessity of viewing the process of adaptation as a flexible, dynamic process rather than assuming a linear progression from Vietnamese to Canadian identity, for example.

Writing of the Indochinese in Australia, Viviani notes the incredible changes that are occurring in refugee families and how stressful these changes can be for individuals and communities. However, she suggests that the refugees' response to these stresses is not simply to try harder to integrate into Australian society:

One common reaction to these changes inside the Indochinese ethnic communities is a reaffirmation of traditional customs and values: in festivals such as lunar New Year and Têt, in emphasis on religion, in reinforcement of native language in ethnic schools, and in attempts to shore up patterns of status and authority in kin and wider groups. (Viviani 1988:190)

McLellan's work on Vietnamese Buddhists in Toronto (1992) also shows the extent to which traditional belief and practice enables refugees to deal with resettlement. Yet increased involvement in religious activities is not necessarily a measure of religiosity among refugees, since Buddhist values and practice can be maintained without communal rituals (at least for one generation). It may take several years for a community to raise enough funds to support a temple and a resident monk. Increased religious activity may not represent a reaffirmation of ethnic identity after a period of attempting to integrate into Canadian society, but rather be the result of the pragmatic fact of finally having enough funds to support a monk. Tran Quang Ba writes of Indochinese in southeastern New Brunswick:

The absence of a pagoda in our region prevents us from knowing if the Buddhists are regular practitioners at home, especially since Vietnamese Buddhism is of the "Great Vehicle" variety (thus different from Cambodian Buddhism which belongs to the "Small Vehicle"), which came from India through China and has less severe religious rules. (Ba 1988:193)

This argument may also reflect the lack of understanding that may exist between Mahayana and Theravada communities or the analyst's bias toward Mahayana Buddhism. From a Mahayana perspective, Buddhist practice may be largely personal and familial practice, but for Theravada communities, monks and temples are critical for maintaining both personal and community practice.

Buchignani argues that for no Indochinese group is religious affiliation their central social identity, although he recognizes that the Lao and Khmer expend their limited resources on developing religious organizations. He further states that Buddhist traditions are based primarily on patterns of personal and familial observance rather than collective ritual. The exceptions he mentions—life cycle and calendrical rituals—cover most Buddhist rituals. Nevertheless, he is correct in noting that the religious practices of Lao and Khmer Buddhists have no precise equivalents in other communities (Buchignani 1988:28).

## Lao Religious Traditions

Since the fourteenth century when Prince Fa Ngum brought texts, monks and the Prabang Buddha image to Lan Xang, lowland Lao (Lao Loum) have followed the beliefs and practices of Theravada Buddhism. The religious tradition of Sri Lanka, Burma, Thailand, Laos and Cambodia, Theravada Buddhism is also known as Southern Buddhism, Buddhism of the Pali canon, the teaching of the elders and the more derogatory Hinayana, the Small Vehicle, in contrast with Mahayana, the Great Vehicle. Generally, Theravada is considered the more conservative tradition, preserving the original basic teachings as recorded in the Pali canon. A Theravadin monk is one who adheres to the 227 rules of the Pali Patimokkha and is a member of a Theravadin ordination tradition (Gombrich 1988:112). Although Theravada Buddhism was never adopted by the Lao Theung (Lao of the mountain sides) or the Lao Soung (Lao of the mountain tops), their animistic beliefs were understood by the lowland Lao, and in fact, Lao state ceremonies recognized the ancient rights of the Lao Theung to the land (O'Connor 1985). However, in the ideal Lao Buddhist order, a just king (*dammaraja*) would rule over Buddhist and non-Buddhist commoners alike. The non-Buddhist Lao were considered to have lower status than Buddhist Lao because they did not have enough good karma to participate in a Buddhist world (J. Van Esterik 1985:150).

Lao religion includes what some analysts refer to as animistic spirit cults. Both Theravadins and their interpreters have offered a wide range of interpretations for the place of spirits in Buddhist belief and practice. For some, the spirits are evidence for arguing that Buddhism is merely a thin veneer over a more pervasive animism. Others stress the continuity in approach to spirits that characterizes the practice of upland animists and lowland Buddhists (Kirsch 1973; Terweil 1975). I have argued that both locality and guardian spirits are part of Buddhist conceptual order and are in fact a vehicle whereby local spirits were integrated into a single Buddhist worldview (P. Van Esterik 1982). But the question as to how aspects of spirit worship fit with Theravada Buddhism is no clearer for Laos than for Thailand, or for that matter any other Theravada Buddhist country. There is general agreement that spirits have an even more essential place in Lao religious practice than in other Theravadin countries, perhaps because of the close relations between upland animists and lowland Buddhist Lao (cf. Reynolds 1978). Ghosts and spirits are interacted with as part of the Buddhist world order. Buddhist scriptures acknowledge the existence of spirits, although scriptures seldom specify the nature of spirits or the extent of their power. In fact, the scriptures provide limited means of protection against spirits in the form of special verses. Guardian spirits of territorial units perform the Buddhist task of clearing potentially dangerous spirits from "civilized" Buddhist order. Guardian spirits were thus incorporated within the political domain of the Kingdom of Laos and are prerequisites for Buddhist social order. The spirit cults and Buddhism together form a structural unity and appear as two separate subsystems only in the models of analysts. The spirit world provides well-being and terrestrial protection through the provision of communal rituals, while Buddhism responds to the essential problems of life, an extratemporal salvation (Gombrich 1988). Understanding Lao religion in the past and the present requires close attention to obeisance owed to the spirit world as well as the system of Theravada Buddhism. The relation between these two systems provides the unique characteristics of Lao religion.

### Politicizing Lao Buddhism

Under French colonialism (1893–1954), Lao rituals began to lose their sacred character, although Buddhism was restored as the official state religion after independence in 1954. The "process of desanctification of the politico-religious order" under colonial rule included utilizing temples for personal ends, appropriating Buddhist objects and interfering with the running of the Sangha (Gunn 1982:82–83). The rituals legitimizing the king's rule and those of princes throughout the country were undermined, as myth and religion generally were marginalized. Consequently, although Buddhism was the official state religion in postcolonial Laos, it served as the basis for traditional Lao values but "was left with no sense of social responsibility in the building of a Lao nationalist identity" (Stuart-Fox and Bucknell 1982:64). Given the ethnic composition of Laos, Buddhism could not really play a central role in Lao nationalism: "A nationalism in Laos that was dependent on Buddhism consequently risked being seen by other groups as a form threatening cultural domination rather than a vehicle of national integration" (Evans 1990:186).

One legacy of the struggle for independence included the undermining of the role of Buddhism in Lao culture. Both the Royal Lao Government and the Pathet Lao (PL) used Buddhism for political ends, as Stuart-Fox and Bucknell document in their analysis of the politicization of the Sangha. "By involving the Sangha in political controversy and social reform, the government and the PL together destroyed the basis of its authority and prestige" (1982:67).

When the Lao People's Democratic Republic (LPDR) was established in 1975, there were an estimated 800 temples and 15,000 monks and novices in Laos (Dommen 1985:149). From 1975 on, the Pathet Lao made use of the Buddhist Sangha to promote the transition to Marxist ideology. Monks were first re-educated and then instructed to communicate the progressive attitudes of the Pathet Lao to the people, popularizing the slogan, "Laos: Peaceful, Independent, Neutral, Democratic, United, and Constantly Progressing" (Stuart-Fox and Bucknell 1982:68).

The Pathet Lao gradually subordinated Buddhism and brought it under party control. This was accomplished in several ways. The two Lao sects (Mahanikai and Thammayut) were unified into the Lao United Buddhist Association, and the Sangha hierarchy was further weakened by smashing the fans of high-ranking monks (Stuart-Fox and Bucknell 1982:72). The canonical Pali texts and the extra canonical texts were revised, pruned and modernized under the auspices of the Lao People's Revolutionary Party (LPRP) to ensure that the content was compatible with Marxism-Leninism (Lafont 1982:155). Monks were instructed to stop teaching about heaven, hell, merit and karma; in short, the heart of popular Buddhism (Stuart-Fox and Bucknell 1982:69). Monastic ritual in the Theravada tradition required all monks and novices to recite the Patimokkha, the monastic regulations of the Vinaya in the Pali canon. The Pathet Lao transformed this core act into a Lao confessional "in which the faults of monks, in particular any failures to follow the party line, were aired and criticized" (Stuart-Fox and Bucknell 1982:72). Not surprisingly, many monks left the order or left the country as refugees.

Since 1975, there have been conflicting reports about the state of Buddhism in Laos, depending partly on the source of the report—from the LPDR or from Lao refugees in Thai camps. In addition, the policies of the LPDR have changed through time. Most sources agree that restrictions on Buddhism were relaxed after 1979. However, the image of the LPDR as discouraging the practice of Buddhism is widespread. Rumors developed abroad concerning the decline of Buddhism in Laos, including the story that monks have been asked to authorize orders for executions. In Thailand, Phra Rajavaramuni cites the rumor

> that no new monks have entered the monasteries as people are not allowed to ordain, while the pre-existing monks are encouraged or indirectly forced to leave the monkhood and that the monks have been utilized by the current regime as political instruments for indoctrinating the people in the new ideology. (Rajavaramuni 1984:80).

At a practical level, cooperation with the communist regime probably prevented the decimation of Buddhism (personal communication, Bruce Matthews 1992).

Since Buddhism proved hard to suppress in Laos, more attention has focused recently on the compatibility of Buddhism and Marxism and the purification of Buddhist practice. Although discussions of the relation between Buddhist and Marxist ideology remain theoretical arguments for Lao refugees, efforts to purify Buddhist practice had a significant affect on Lao Buddhists both within Laos and overseas.

Individuals in a number of Theravadin countries have attempted to reconcile the contradictions between Buddhism and Marxism, either for the purposes of rhetoric or for guidance in constructing a socialist state. In Laos, the LPRP portrayed the Buddha as an early pre scientific revolutionary (Dommen 1985:151). Elsewhere, when Marxists were brought into a coalition government in Sri Lanka in 1964, a Theravadin monk said that "The Buddha was the greatest

Marxist in the world" (Smith 1971:150). Socialists stress that both Marxism and Buddhism assume the equality of individuals. In defending the compatibility of Buddhism and socialism, a Lao monk argued that Buddhism is compatible with a number of different social systems, once Buddhism is purged of rituals and superstitions that served the old order (Stuart-Fox and Bucknell 1982:69). In 1976, the minister of education, sports and religious Affairs argued that "revolutionary politics and the politics practiced by the Lord Buddha have the same goals. They differ only in organization and practice" (Stuart-Fox and Bucknell 1982:69). Thai Marxists, perhaps because they are not putting their rhetoric into practice, argue that Buddhism and Marxism are compatible but that Buddhism as a useful social doctrine was distorted by the ruling class (Wedel 1987:105). They, too, have argued the need to purge Buddhism of its animistic and Brahmanistic elements. However, rather than think out the basic assumptions underlying Marxism and Buddhism—their views of causality, of the nature of human existence and of the nature of the rewards of each system—attention has been focused on how to strip Buddhist practice of its undesirable elements. In Laos, these undesirable elements have included conspicuous merit making and spirit worship.

Conspicuous merit making, ostensibly linked to support of the Sangha but equally linked to the maintenance of social position, was strongly discouraged by the LPDR for both economic and ideological reasons. The party attempted to stop people giving rice to the monks on their morning rounds, but the order was later relaxed because it was deeply resented by the Lao. When the party tried to regulate the amount and timing of household donations, there was a general feeling that giving rice in this way no longer amounted to a meritorious act (Dommen 1985:152). Giving (*dana*) must be done freely and with good intentions to make merit. Being ordered when to give and how much is, in theory, a much more effective way to undercut Buddhist values than forbidding donations to monks altogether.

Like Burma in its war against the *nats* (spirits) in the 1960s, the LPDR acted to purge Lao Buddhists of superstitions such as belief in guardian spirits. Evans (1990:187) argues that the exodus of monks from village temples actually led to a revival of spirit worship at the village level. But even more than in other Theravadin countries, belief in territorial guardian spirits of units such as villages, provincial centers and the nation state represents the structural basis of Lao belief through a system of *emboîtment* or encasing (cf. Condominas 1978:106, O'Connor 1985; P. Van Esterik 1982). Thus, the prosperity of the Lao kingdom was guaranteed not only by the rule of a Buddhist righteous monarch (a *dhammaraja*), but also by offerings to the myriad of territorially based guardian spirits and the palladium of the nation state, the Prabang. This Buddha image originated in Sri Lanka and was taken by Prince Fa Ngum from Angkor Wat to Luang Prabang in the early fourteenth century when it was revered as the most sacred Buddha image in the nation.

When Lao refugees leave Laos, they lose the protection of these territorially based guardian spirits. Even where Buddhist institutions are reestablished, there is no substitute within the refugee camps in Thailand or the apartments of Toronto for the territorially based guardian spirits of Laos. The cults of the guardian spirits threaten the LPDR more than institutional Buddhism threatens it; for the essential Buddhist concepts can be made compatible with some aspects of Marxist theory, while territorially based guardian spirits harken back to the embeddedness of royal Lao rituals and the long-established patron-client relationships undermined by the LPDR.

Contemporary Lao Buddhism as practiced in Laos and North America have two features in common: in both locations, spirit worship and conspicuous merit making are radically altered from their forms in prerevolutionary Laos. Yet both were key elements in the practice of traditional Lao Buddhism. Ironically, while rituals concerning locality spirits have all but disappeared in North America, the need for personal protection and personal guardians may have increased as refugee families face seen and unseen dangers in North America. (cf. Muecke 1987) Thus, rituals such as the *soukhouan* (or *baci*) that strengthen individuals' capacity to withstand potentially disruptive experiences continue to be important.

The description of Lao rituals in Toronto (Chapter Four) demonstrates how merit-making patterns must be altered to fit with life in an urban North American context. While the motivation for and the form of merit making in North American communities may closely resemble traditional Lao patterns, the strategies for arranging rituals in Toronto or Montreal or Washington differ substantially. As in postrevolutionary practice, food giving must be ordered in some way to ensure that the monks are provided for every day and so that people who come from substantial distances to feed the monks can be assured that their gifts can be ritually accepted. The dual problems of too little food and too much food require some form of regulation in North American communities.

The parallels between the revolutionary efforts to purify, simplify and use Buddhism for their own ends and the refugees' efforts to re-establish a form of Buddhism appropriate for a Judeo-Christian context will be developed further in Chapter Six.

Lao refugees arriving in North America saw Buddhist practices in Laos discouraged since 1975, or earlier than 1975 if they came from Pathet Lao–controlled areas. Lao refugees nineteen years old and younger are unlikely to have ever participated in Buddhist community rituals. Lao in North America who are now in their twenties and thirties saw community rituals ridiculed or politicized when they were at a most impressionable age. Consequently, a generation of Lao refugees in North America have no direct experience with community-based Lao Buddhism and must reinvent a community-based practice from the experiences of their elders, their perceived needs and the Buddhist resources in their new surroundings.

Individual and community responses to this situation include the decision to reject religion altogether, to privatize or internalize its practice, to secularize religion until it resembles community cultural events or to convert to Christianity.

### Repositioning Religion

Lao Buddhism was never compartmentalized as a separate domain in Laos: it was an essential part of daily life. In North America, religious belief and practice is a very distinct domain, usually seen as detached or detachable from other parts of life. For many Lao refugees, religion itself may become an irrelevant domain. Constrained by time, financial resources and knowledge of Buddhist practice, after years in refugee camps, religion in general and Buddhism in particular may cease to be relevant to everyday life in North America.

There is very little evidence in the social science literature concerning religiosity among refugees. Most ethnographers would probably reject as inaccurate any survey answers regarding degree of religious beliefs. Similarly, the Lao survey question asking whether Buddhism is less important, more important, or of the same importance for the respondent in Laos and Canada is more suggestive than meaningful: 10.8 percent responded that Buddhism was less important now, 12.9 percent responded that Buddhism was more important now and 76.3 percent responded that Buddhism had the same importance for them in Laos and in Canada. A monk, in answer to a similar question, made little distinction between the needs of his congregation in Washington, D.C., and in Laos. He saw these needs as

> more or less the same as in Laos. They come to the temple because they are happy to do it. It provides fulfillment. Their problems depend on income, education, types of jobs, family, a new life. I can give them advice about all of these kinds of problem. (Coudoux 1985:32).

When there are no monks available in a community to provide counseling and ritual services, there is no reason to assume that the Lao are no longer practicing Buddhists. For example, 81.6 percent of respondents said that they prayed at home, 34.6 percent meditated and 38.5 percent kept eight precepts on certain days. Of course, these responses are from a sample of Lao who are already committed to Buddhist practice, since they were attending a service when the survey was distributed. These are all successful, short-term individual strategies for maintaining Buddhism as a system of ethics and morality. However, these strategies do not address the long-term need to teach Buddhism as a total religious system to the younger generation.

Buchignani (1988:28) states that Buddhist traditions are based primarily on patterns of personal and familial observance rather than collective ritual . This perpetuates widely held western stereotypes about Buddhism as an esoteric individual practice. Although personal and household observances are part of both Theravada and Mahayana practice, collective ritual is important in both.

The decision to hold individual and household observances is an adaptive strategy for Buddhists who have no access to monks and temples. The lack of religious specialists in many Canadian communities makes it difficult to practice collectively. Two other obstacles blocking participation in religious services are lack of transportation and lack of time because individuals often work at two or more jobs (Venerable Uparatana 1989:50). But the efforts individuals and communities expend on communal rituals when an opportunity presents itself confirms that collective rituals are an integral part of Buddhist practice.

When monks are not available, individuals with substantial experience in ritual may lead a small number of adults in prayer services at their homes. The initiative is usually taken by elderly refugees who have both the time and the need to increase their Buddhist involvement, as occurred in Victoria (Woon et al. 1988:59). In Theravadin countries, devout laypersons may memorize the Pali chants and recite the same services as monks do. But laypersons are not fields of merit for other laypersons and act only out of individual piety and compassion. Nevertheless, these older persons are valuable resources in communities without monks (or where other laity have forgotten responses because the community has been without monks and services for so long).

Yet Buddhists may also be oriented toward personal morality rather than collective merit making. Those individuals socialized in this manner may adapt best to a religious landscape with few practitioners. With a small Buddha altar in the house, individuals and families may recite the refuges and undertake to follow the precepts by reciting the same chants as the monks use. When emphasizing personal morality, meditation, prayer and taking five or eight precepts, individuals have less need for monks and temples.

But this route to Buddhist practice and salvation is open mainly to adult Lao and Khmer adepts who have spent many years in a practicing Buddhist community. Although adult men who have been monks and some adult women may follow this route, the option is more problematic for the young Lao who have grown up in refugee camps.

I asked a monk in Bangkok about the religious options available to Buddhist refugees in North America, and his answer reflects the attitude of those Thai intellectuals who are turning away from lavish merit making rituals. He said, "The core of Buddhism is personal morality and meditation. Monks are not needed." But for older Lao and Khmer refugees fleeing from peasant villages, communal merit-making rituals were the basis of Buddhist practice. Without monks and without previous training in meditation or enough education to read relevant texts, it is difficult to see how adults could maintain Buddhist practice, let alone how youngsters could develop practice. Young people learn about personal morality and the concepts motivating meditation through communal ritual, unlike westerners who pick up meditation practice as a discrete activity often more related to mental health and stress reduction than to Buddhist practice. Even in places like Toronto where the Lao Buddhist ritual tradition exists—albeit transformed and sporadic--teenagers have to be told what to say and do during services, and few know what the ritual occasions celebrate let alone the chants appropriate for the occasion.

**Secularization and Conversion**

"We want to conserve our culture, our festivals, our dances, our music, our religion" (Simon-Barouh 1983:171). In writing of the Cambodians in Rennes, France, Simon-Barouh outlines the efforts the Cambodians have made to preserve their ancestral culture for their children and to encourage solidarity, " motivated by the desire not to remain a lost people, even in exile" (Simon-Barouh 1983:22). Here, Buddhist religion is treated as a marker of ethnic identity to be preserved. Preservation is encouraged by the fact that Buddhist celebrations such as the New Year and the Festival of the Dead (September or October) become the focal point for a communal celebration and meal; for a few hours, "it's a happy occasion, just like back home," as they "recreate and experience the atmosphere of Cambodia in an underground parking facility or in the basement of a housing project on the outskirts of the city" (Simon-Barouh 1983:20).

Religion—Buddhism, for many Lao refugees in North America—has become equated with tradition, and tradition is defined by such things as eating Lao food, listening to Lao music, wearing Lao fabrics and celebrating a few annual ceremonies such as Lao New Year. These celebrations can be carried out even if there is no resident monk. For many communities of Southeast Asian refugees there are no local practitioners who can arrange regular Buddhist services, but a great number of adults can organize wonderful social and cultural events.

Both Lao and Thai in Toronto and elsewhere in North America face the problem of balancing the need for "religious" resources and "cultural" resources. There is often a much greater demand for a cultural center where children can take language, dance or other classes relating to their ethnic heritage, where newspapers and magazines from home are available and where lavish parties can be held celebrating national holidays. These national holidays may coincide with the celebration of Buddhist ceremonies. However, the national celebrations reveal tensions between Buddhism as a marker of ethnicity and Buddhism as a system of beliefs and practices.

In Toronto, the Lao associations are sensitive about the potential divisions between Lao Buddhists and Lao Christians. To counteract these divisive tendencies, secular Lao festivals are encouraged, such as community dinners, dances and sports events coinciding with what would be Buddhist festivals in Laos. By reducing the visibility of the Buddhist elements, the community reduces the basis for factionalism

The existence of cultural centers as opposed to temples attests to the need for strategic planning on the part of ethnic minorities who may be forced to redefine certain activities as "cultural" rather than "religious" to secure funding. Yet the secularization of festivals does not solve the problem for Buddhists who are oriented toward merit making and Buddhist practice.

In spite of the tensions within some Lao communities, Lao Buddhists stress that Christianity and Buddhism can easily coexist because they share similar ethics and moral teachings. In movies such as the University of Northern Illinois's *Rebirth of a Culture*, the Lao argue that there should be no conflict between the religions. In fact, many of them attend Buddhist merit-making services on Saturday and Christian services on Sunday. Ebihara points out similarities between Buddhism and Christianity:

Both religions emphasize the importance of moral, harmonious, and compassionate conduct toward others. Both have "commandments" for behavior that prohibit killing, stealing, lying, and nonmarital sexual relations. Both have a round of annual holidays that are occasions for sermons, prayers, and offerings, as well as festive gatherings of relatives and friends. The Buddhist temple . . . resembles the church or synagogue in being both a religious and a social center for the congregants. . .(Ebihara 1985:140)

But these are broad structural similarities between the practice of Buddhism and the practice of Christianity that mask incredible differences in logic and beliefs. The Lao are generally uninterested in analyzing the historical or epistemological bases of the two traditions. However, they are very much aware of the social and political implications following from the decision to participate in Christian or Buddhist activities. The pragmatic decisions have considerable ramifications for refugees, particularly if they are sponsored by church groups.

Lao Buddhists who convert to Christianity in refugee camps or after resettlement are not the focus of this study. In fact, the focus on Lao Buddhism makes it difficult to address questions of conversion and reconversion or the complexities of Buddhist-Christian dialogue. Other studies address these issues from the Christian perspective (cf. Winland 1992 for a discussion of Hmong Mennonites). However, this was a sensitive issue during fieldwork, as any discussion of Christianity within the context of Buddhist services reinforced the suspicion that I might be a missionary trying to convert Buddhists to Christian beliefs.

Approximately 500 Lao in Toronto consider themselves to be Christian, and most converted in the camps. They are strongly linked to the churches and are given transportation to the services and encouraged to bring other Lao with them. Of the 111 survey respondents who were asked if they had ever attended a Christian church service in Canada, 19 respondents declined to answer. Of those who answered, 44.6 percent said they had attended a Christian service.

Buddhist-Christian dialogue is well established in western religious studies (cf. the journal *Buddhist Christian Studies* from the University of Hawaii). As one scholar notes, "Buddhists and Christians have not slaughtered each other with the same gusto that other religions employed in dealing with each other" (McAteer 1988:10). This tolerance is growing as more Christians and Jews become interested in Buddhist meditation techniques. But the borrowing of specific techniques of practice does not imply understanding, tolerance or even necessarily knowledge of Buddhist *dhamma*. The Venerable Khantipalo Thera expressed the situation of many westerners who meditate as practicing *dhamma* without Buddha and *sangha*. Khantipalo criticizes those who revere the Buddha as a teacher but ignore the teachings and the order; those who separate out a "method" like *vipassana* meditation for practice but ignore the Buddha and *sangha;* and those—primarily westerners—who revere special teachers as "gurus" but ignore the Buddha as teacher and the *Dhamma* beyond the practices taught by their teachers (Khantipalo 1988:15). One American Buddhist felt that Buddhism was being dismantled or cannibalized: "Without *Sila* (ethics), without the development of the *Paramis* (the perfections of behavior), meditation practice can be as self-serving as any other pursuit" (Bernstein 1989:117).

Relations between Buddhism and Christianity and between Buddhists and Christians raise many important questions that cannot be addressed here. These questions require separate examination, beginning with ethnographic research among Lao Christians. There are probably a few Lao Christians who were converted long before they entered the refugee camps and resettled in North America. Protestant missionaries have been active in Laos since the 1920s. For example, one group of Christian Lao in Vancouver are led by a Lao pastor who comes from a line of pastors including the first Christian convert in Laos, his grandfather (Placzek 1987:8). Analysis is further complicated by the practice of describing Buddhism in terms of Christian categories when writing in English. This vocabulary includes such terms as *monks, lent, Sabbath, Sunday School, priest, nun, services* and *holy water.*

For those Lao who choose to remain Buddhist and seek to practice their religion communally, there is no alternative but to work to recreate suitable Buddhist institutions in North America. To do this, communities must attract and retain one or more Lao monks. The following chapter demonstrates the efforts of one Lao community to establish a Lao temple in Toronto.

# Chapter Four

## Creating Wat Lao

### The Search for a Resident Monk

Resident monks at an official Buddhist temple are necessary for a long-term    solution to the problem of being a Buddhist in a Judeo-Christian society. But choosing, attracting and supporting a Lao monk in a North American city are all complex undertakings fraught with practical and political problems. For the Lao, monks are very important for regular merit-making activities and for teaching Buddhist essentials to their children. They are therefore ready to expend great amounts of energy, time and money to establish Wat Lao (Lao temple).

Criteria for choosing a monk are not openly discussed, since any monk who keeps his vows is a suitable field of merit for lay devotees. Informally, however, it is clear that Lao Buddhists, as well as Theravada Buddhists from other countries, constantly evaluate monks on a number of different dimensions. There is agreement that a senior monk is preferable to a junior monk, but few senior monks are resettled in North America. The longer a man has been in the monkhood, the better he knows the ritual procedures and a wide range of Pali chants. Some refugees spoke of "men in yellow robes" who were ordained either in Laos or in the refugee camps in hopes of gaining protection as refugees or of being resettled overseas. In the confusion of the late 1970s in Laos, there were a number of "fake monks" who never were ordained at all. Bringing a senior monk to North America gives the Lao confidence that they have a serious monk ordained legitimately in Laos or Thailand and worth the incredible efforts necessary to bring him from the refugee camps.

Ideally, the monk chosen should be a scholar capable of teaching about Buddhism. As a possessor of wisdom, he would be appropriate for socializing children born in the camps or in Canada into their Buddhist heritage. But wisdom is also obtained through meditation. Lao monks in Thailand from forest monasteries are particularly revered as meditation masters. They are greatly respected by both Thai immigrants and westerners who seek meditation training. While Thai immigrants and western converts might well benefit by bringing such a meditation adept, such a monk might not be able to address the daily pastoral needs of a rural Lao refugee population or be able to teach "Buddhist Sunday School." Buddhist texts and practices provide models for a wide variety of monastic styles—scholar monks, pastoral monks, activist monks, meditation monks and monks considered to have magical powers. In North America, it is also useful to have a monk who could speak English or French well enough to be useful in communicating with non-Lao.

Thus, at every stage in the selection process, members of the Lao Buddhist Association and other interested community members must weigh these different factors, relying on relatives in Laos and in Thai camps to identify likely candidates. But refugees also expressed concern that after all these efforts to bring someone to Canada, the monk might not be content to stay in the monkhood and the community. At a Lao merit-making ceremony in a small apartment, a few men quietly prepared strategies on how to arrange for two monks to leave the refugee camps in Thailand and take up residence in Toronto. "But what if we sponsor him and he leaves the monkhood after he arrives here?" asked one man with great concern. Immigration officials in Bangkok are very much aware that a monk may leave his vocation after being admitted as a refugee.

After finding a suitable monk in the camp, there are real questions about removing a monk from a setting where he is so obviously needed. There, thousands of Lao sit in makeshift and temporary shelters that are becoming permanent residences for many who have been in the camps for over ten years. There, anything that relieves the apathy and anxiety of camp life is critical to refugees who have been "marking time" for years.

Further, when more Lao are repatriated, there may be a place for monks who were ordained before 1975, as LPDR now allows freedom of religious expression. From many perspectives, the need may be greater within the refugee camps than in the northern suburbs of Toronto. For refugee selection committees in Thailand, the decision is not a simple one, and the loss of a monk from a refugee camp is a difficult compromise.

Having found a monk who is willing to immigrate to Canada, the next hurdle is the immigration process. From the point of view of the selection committee, many potential candidates are viewed as refugees with little schooling and few marketable skills useful in Canada. Further, they are unlikely to speak English or French or have any great interest in trying to learn the languages, for they are among the very few refugees in camps who have a clear function and can fill their days with activities that continue to have meaning for them and their communities. They are among the fortunate few who have meaningful work. Nevertheless, to immigration officials they are unlikely to become successfully established when they arrive in Canada. The immigration officials consider "a person's fluency in English or French, any employment skills they possess and their educational level," as well as "family size, relatives or others in Canada who may be able to help in their settlement, and the degree of motivation and initiative displayed since the person has arrived in Thailand" (Hardinge 1988:2:14).

Consequently, the refugees who are least likely to become dependent on the Canadian government are often rejected as government-sponsored refugees because they are viewed as unskilled. Private sponsorship is the only route for most refugee monks to enter Canada. This takes time, substantial money and familiarity with Canadian immigration procedures.

But of all refugees, monks are the least likely to ever become dependent on government or welfare as long as they remain monks. Local Lao communities provide the prerequisites for life in Canadian cities. For example, before the first monk arrived in Toronto, the Lao Buddhist Association had collected over six thousand dollars; found apartment accommodation; organized medical insurance; purchased bedding, dishes and all household equipment; and arranged for long-term support for transportation and daily food.

These are formidable tasks for newly arrived refugees to accomplish. Moreover, funding has continually been forthcoming for unanticipated expenses. Donations are substantial, even from families who work double shifts in factories to meet their own living expenses. The experience gained in handling these bureaucratic tasks, organizing working committees and establishing effective leadership will, no doubt, have a synergistic effect on other Lao undertakings in Canada.

### Financing and Provisioning Wat Lao

Since the Lenten season (Pali: *Vassa*) in 1985, at least one Lao monk has been resident at Wat Lao more or less continuously in Toronto. In spite of all the difficulties in funding, provisioning and locating a Lao Buddhist temple in Toronto, Wat Lao of Ontario is now registered as a religious association and participates in the Buddhist Council of Canada.

The first resident monk came from Montreal. After a period in Toronto, he answered the request of the Lao community in Winnipeg to set up a Wat Lao there. A second monk came from Montreal to reside in Toronto for the Lenten season. The Montreal community was reluctant to have this particular monk leave Montreal permanently, but they have provided another monk to reside permanently in Toronto. In addition, monks from other communities come occasionally when invited by Wat Lao.

In December 1988, Wat Lao moved to a new location in a complex of apartment buildings in the Jane-Finch area. The small apartment uses the living/dining-room area to receive guests. The altar and mats are arranged for worship for small groups. For more than a dozen or so, especially for ritual occasions, the temple committee arranges hall rentals. The new apartment was purchased for $124,000. The old apartment, on the top floor of an apartment complex at Keele and Caledonia, was sold at a small profit to a Lao family. The Lao Buddhist Association could have made more money on the sale, but were primarily concerned with making a convenient transaction, housing the Lao family and starting to save for land for a new Wat Lao--a place where an ordination hall could be constructed and a full chapter of monks housed. The dream of a fully equipped temple in Toronto competes with the more easily expressed (and more fundable) need for a community center.

Having a monk resident at Wat Lao permits members of the Lao community to make merit on a regular basis by offering food and donations to the monk and by listening to chants and sermons (*dhamma* or teachings). Although

Tambiah (1970) and others have stressed the reciprocal relation between monks and laity in Southeast Asian communities, the exchange is very different in the cities of North America. In Laos, households provide sons to be ordained for varying lengths of time, and the task of provisioning monks is spread evenly through the community. In North America, monks are extremely rare and difficult to replace. Ordinations take place only with the greatest expenditure of effort into an ordination tradition of questionable legitimacy. It is much more expensive to support a monk in a North American city than in a Lao village temple. Consequently, merit-making occasions are rare compared with opportunities in Laos.

Wat Lao receives an extraordinary amount of food on ritual occasions. Other days, it would be possible that no food at all would be presented to the monks. This swing between an excess and potential dearth of food is characteristic of many Theravada temples in North America. It is the responsibility of the temple committee to handle food donations in such a way as to ensure that food is regularly donated but at the same time provide the opportunity for spontaneous or unexpected merit making through food donations. A few households in the same apartment building as Wat Lao provide food on a regular basis. Other families phone in for appointments to provide food on certain days.

Food, money, sets of incense, flowers and candles are the donations given by almost everyone attending a Lao Buddhist ceremony. But the act of giving money is not a simple transaction in the context of Lao Buddhism. For example, almost all cash is handed from one person to another so that merit is shared more widely. This is done with simplicity and grace, as bills are passed among family and friends and visitors. Women initiate much of the communal giving. During one ritual, a woman passed a twenty-dollar bill through several people to her husband sitting near the front of the hall. She then kept after him, watching him carefully to make sure he donated the money. Glancing back over his shoulder at his wife, he reluctantly placed the bill on the pedestal dish in front of the monk.

Donations during ceremonies are carefully divided into contributions to Wat Lao to cover current expenses such as rent, medical insurance; and supplies, contributions toward the purchase of land and the building of a real temple in the area; and gifts to individual monks. Money for monks is handled by the temple committee on behalf of the monk.

Money is collected separately for sermons. Donations from individuals are placed in offering bowls before the sermon is recited. If the temple committee does not consider the amount sufficient, then extra funds will be taken from general donations to the temple to cover the amount. This is particularly important if the monk has come from out of town.

Dividing donations into distinct categories is carried out spontaneously during the services. For example, during one service, a woman donated one dollar to a family presenting a tray of food to the monks in the name of a deceased relative (the name of the relative was written on a piece of paper and burned over water before the tray of food was presented to the monk), one dollar to another family collecting donations to cover the cost of a set of new robes for the monk, one dollar for the sermon and one dollar to Wat Lao.

At every community ritual, members of the temple committee give a detailed accounting of the expenses and donations to the temple. When the new Wat Lao was formed, the financial report to the community included the total income from ceremonies and donations over the past two years ($6,690.70), the cost to register the Lao Buddhist Association ($70.00), the first and last months' rent for the monk's apartment ($1,115.00), items purchased for the monk ($82.91) and other costs such as transportation and health insurance. At the end of the service, they announced the names of donors to the temple and the items donated and gave the total amount donated that day to Ban Napho refugee camp in Thailand.

The financial burdens for establishing a Lao temple in Toronto are substantial and are not borne equally across the whole population. About 10 percent to 15 percent of the Lao population of Toronto attend Buddhist celebrations regularly. The social events and sports events draw a much larger number of Lao.

Although no direct question regarding income was asked in the survey, it is likely that financial security is not common among Lao refugees in Toronto. About 60 percent of the respondents are either unemployed or working as skilled or unskilled laborers. A quarter of the respondents only completed the first four grades of elementary school in Laos, hardly enough to maintain literacy. The majority of these are women.

Nevertheless, the community shoulders the financial responsibility of Wat Lao through the practice of merit-making. Most merit-making donations include cash. Table 4.1 illustrates where most of these financial donations were made. Most respondents applied their donations to more than one location.

**Table 4.1.Location of Temple Donations**

| City | % of Respondents |
| --- | --- |
| Toronto | 93.9 |
| Montreal | 27.9 |
| Other Canadian city | 17.1 |
| United States | 36.9 |
| Sent to Thailand | 19.8 |
| Sent to Laos | 20.7 |

Before Toronto had a resident monk, the temple committee negotiated with the Buddhist Association of Montreal to bring a monk to visit Toronto. The Lao in Toronto would contribute toward the food and transportation of the monk and would give about 20 percent of the donations received to the temple in Montreal. Many of the survey respondents who answered that they donated money to Montreal may actually have donated the money in Toronto, for the Lao in Toronto do not generally contribute support to the Montreal temple when they have a resident monk in Toronto.

When resident monks are available, the seasonal round of merit-making ceremonies are celebrated in Toronto. Attention is focused on the more important religious occasions, where laity can gain more merit (Suksamran 1977:9). The seasonal round of ceremonies reflects the biography of the historical Buddha—Wisaka Puja (day of birth, enlightenment, and death of the Buddha), Khao Phansa (entering Lent) and Ok Phansa (leaving Lent)— as well as periodic yearly ceremonies such as *Songkran* (traditional New Year).

In addition, monks participate in household merit-making activities, such as housewarmings and memorials for deceased relatives.

## Rituals in Toronto

Descriptions of the following rituals are based on participant observation on one or more occasions. In addition, for most occasions I had the assistance of my husband, John, who recorded observations and conversed more directly with Lao men, and a Thai assistant with knowledge of the Lao language and long-term familiarity with Buddhist rituals.

### Precept Day, Wan Sin

The combination of chants and prayers that make up the core of Lao Buddhist ceremonies in Toronto are built from the morning worship that monks would have recited in Laos every day. On Buddhist holy days (Thai: *wan phra*; Lao: *wan sin*) that occur on the quarters of the lunar month, the laity join in the service and present offerings of food to the monks (Thai: *tak bat*). All the periodic rituals of the Buddhist calendar year build on this service. Rather than repeat the ritual sequence of every service, I will first describe the formal structure of *wan sin,* giving some descriptive context, and later identify the special characteristics of other rituals that build from this basic morning service. Following the description of a typical precept day and another key ritual act, *soukhouan,* I will review a number of communal calendrical celebrations and individual noncalendrical celebrations such as ordination that the Lao celebrate in Toronto.

Although the *wan sin* "order of service" is similar in Laos and Canada, the occasion itself is quite different in Canada. Only 29 percent of survey respondents indicated they attended *wan sin* services in Canada. This may be a problem of translation, although the temple committee approved the translation and transcription of terms. The low response to this question may demonstrate that in North America, no "ordinary" *wan sin* can be celebrated because of the need to shift *wan sin* services to Sunday. Because of the rarity of ritual events, few *wan sin* services may be celebrated without other rituals being "tagged on." That is, communal rituals may only be undertaken on the *wan sin* that coincide with more significant Buddhist occasions.

Services are often videotaped from the entry of the monks to the end of the announcements at the end of the service to have a record of ritual occasions. This taping is done for most important ritual celebrations, particularly such unique occasions as a son's ordination or the visit of a famous monk. The monks from Wat Lao Buddhavong in Washington, D.C., use videos as a means of recording and therefore protecting Lao culture for future generations (Coudoux 1985:41).

*Wan sin* is usually celebrated on Sundays at Wat Lao, but a community hall is rented when large numbers of worshippers are expected. The following description captures the stable features of these Lao Buddhist services.

Members of the temple committee come early to clean the hall, lay down Lao mats and prepare the altar. Often a low platform is built to hold the table displaying the Buddha image, flowers, incense and candles and the cushions for the monks. There is a festive air, much chatting and catching up with news of relatives and friends.

Around 9:00 A.M., families begin to assemble, the women dressed in Lao sarongs (*pha sin*) and stoles (*pha biang*), the men in suits and most of the children in western-style casual clothes. All remove their shoes at the door. The men congregate around the community leaders or the monk, if he is there early. The women deliver their cooked food dishes to the kitchen, where they are distributed among trays to be offered to the monks and later consumed by the laity. They arrange their offerings to be put directly in the monks' begging bowls in ornate aluminum pedestal bowls purchased from Thailand and available at local Lao grocery stores in Toronto. These offerings include sticky glutinous rice stored in small, round baskets, fruit and wrapped desserts such as cookies or Twinkies.

The noise level in the hall rises as women from different communities have an opportunity to exchange family news. When one or more monks enter the hall, the Lao nearest his path pay their respects with folded hands and bowed head (*wai*), but the conversation continues as before. Both men and women may proceed to the platform, making sure to keep their heads lower than the monk's, make obeisance three times and privately chat with the monk, asking advice, requesting help or inviting him to a service at their homes.

About 10:00 A.M., the men arrange themselves cross-legged on the mats in front of the monk, the old women with their legs folded to one side directly behind the men and younger women and children at the back. A few men and teenagers remain at the back of the hall or sit on the chairs near the back, but most indicate their intention to participate by sitting on the mats, hands folded, and occasionally chanting along with the monks. Children may quiet down themselves and sit with their mothers. The occasional youngster will continue walking on the mats, stepping over the offering bowls and bumping into adults deep in prayer, without reprimand.

A layman with knowledge of the Pali chants invites the monk (or monks) to give the precepts and refuges to the congregation. The monk chants the Pali verses into a microphone with the laity repeating the words, the older men and women loudly and confidently, the younger almost silently. Next, the laity repeat the refuges and the recitation of the five precepts (an agreement to honor the vows for one day).

### Three Refuges

I come to the Lord Buddha, the Dharma and the Order for refuge and reflection: they truly expel suffering and danger to the end of life.

For the second time I come to the Lord Buddha, the Dharma and the Order of refuge and reflection: they truly expel suffering and danger to the end of life.

For the third time I come to the Lord Buddha, the Dharma and the Order for refuge and reflection: they truly expel suffering and danger to the end of life.

### Five Precepts

I beg to observe the precept—refrain from taking life
I beg to observe the precept—refrain from taking what is not given
I beg to observe the precept—abstain from improper sexual pleasures
I beg to observe the precept—refrain from speaking falsehoods
I beg to observe the precept—refrain from drinking intoxicants.

(after Wells 1960:53)

While most of the laity know these chants by heart, many are not familiar with other Pali chants, such as those that invite all deities to assemble and hear the *dhamma* (teachings). These chants are repeated only by men who have been monks or by especially devout older women.

Following these chants, the monks repeat *sathu* ("well done") three times and prepare to accept the food offerings the laity have prepared for them. To the sound of Lao music over the loudspeakers, the highest-ranking males file up with the pedestal bowls their wives and mothers have prepared for them and place some sticky rice sweets, fruit and donations of flowers, incense, candles and money in or beside each of the monks' begging bowls. Slowly, all men, women and children file up in turn to repeat the process. Silently but efficiently, the men of the temple committee take the offerings out of the bowls and sort them out into green garbage bags to allow the entire congregation, often 300 or more people, to place offerings directly in the small begging bowls of the monks.

The monks then touch the bowls and trays of food that have been prepared in the kitchen and offered to them by senior men. They accept the gifts of the laity by chanting a Pali verse (*sangha bhithuti*). At the end of their meal, the monks chant the *anumodana*, or the verse to share merit with all sentient beings. For the Lao, this appears to be the most sacred and emotionally charged moment of the service. Men and women take out small bottles of water, and with the left hand raised to the head, bowing low, they slowly pour the water into their pedestal bowls (*kruat nam*, the sharing of merit through water). By this act, they transfer merit to all sentient beings, most consciously to their deceased relatives in Laos, by the power of words spoken by the monks (cf. J. Van Esterik 1977:88). The canonical basis for merit transfer is discussed in more detail by Gombrich (1988:124–27) and J. Van Esterik (1977:95–102). The act may be interpreted differently by some refugees who suggested that sharing merit would help them find lost loved ones and be reunited with them.

Members of the Lao Buddhist Association and Wat Lao may announce other services, make speeches or introduce a sermon to take place later while the monks eat. Inevitably, the temple committee will make a detailed breakdown of all financial contributions to the temple identifying the amount of the donation and the name of the donor. The timing of the announcements and the sermon may shift depending on the ritual occasion.

Generally, everyone who has participated in the service shares in consuming the food that has been accepted or blessed by the monks. Groups of a dozen or so friends and relatives gather around a tray of dishes and baskets of sticky rice, and enjoy the most authentic Lao food they may consume that week. The dishes presented are the most time-consuming to prepare and contain fresh Lao herbs available only in one or two Lao grocery stores downtown. For Lao teenagers, this may be their only opportunity to sample the full range of dishes so fondly remembered by their elders in the days when Buddhist celebrations provided structure and meaning to Lao village life. On the other hand, some families bring take-out hamburgers for their children to eat. The children are particularly interested in the Twinkies and chocolate cupcakes offered to the monks and redistributed to the less discriminating young laity.

As families begin to gather up their dishes, shoes and children to make the trip home, temple committee members pull apart flower offerings, separating incense and candles into bags and money, earmarked for maintenance of the temple or other merit-making purposes, into envelopes. The mats are rolled up, the altar dismantled and returned to the small apartment-temple, and the hall returns to its barren shabby appearance.

### *Soukhouan*

If *wan sin* is the core activity of Theravada Buddhist practice in Laos and for Lao on North America, *soukhouan* rituals, which often accompany Buddhist, community and household celebrations, express the core of Lao values. Despite the disruption in Laos and the changes in the lives of Lao refugees, this ritual practice condenses what it means to be Lao—particularly a Lao among other Lao, for it is a ritual celebrating social relatedness in a concrete and powerful way.

The following descriptions of Lao rituals often refer to *baci* or *soukhouan* rituals, which form a significant part of a number of ceremonial occasions occurring in North American communities. *Soukhouan* ceremonies are integral to most Lao celebrations at the household and community level.

*Soukhouan* rituals literally invite the thirty-two components of an individual's spirit essence or *khouan* to reside comfortably and permanently in an individual. If the *khouan* left the body for any length of time, physical or mental illness or even death might result. The *khouan* is thought to reside in the hair whorls on the crown of the head. The term *khouan* is often glossed in English as "soul," a very "un-Buddhist" term. There is no Buddhist equivalent of the Hindu concept of *atman*, or soul. The integration of a concept like spirit essence or *khouan* into Buddhist cosmology is an exceptionally complex question at least partially dealt with by Tambiah (1970:57–59), but its meaning as spirit essence of a person is unproblematic to the Lao.

The term *soukhouan* is in most general use; the term *baci* refers specifically to the conical tray-like structure for the "auspicious rice" used in the ritual. The Cambodian origin of the word hints at the more formal or royal context of the term *baci*, compared to the more general informal term *soukhouan*. While the lavish *baci* of kings and princes may have clear Brahmanical elements, the core of *soukhouan* was clearly pre-Brahmanic, pre-Buddhist and indigenous Tai. Tai peoples shared a common ritual language of mobile "souls" and locality spirits. Perhaps because of the ethnic complexity of Laos and the fact that it was less politically integrated into a centralized state system, the various locality spirits were never "upgraded" to Brahman gods as in Thailand, nor were they effectively "Buddhaized." Thus, Lao locality spirits may have been less anchored and less controlled than comparable Thai spirits (P. Van Esterik 1982).

These linguistic usages suggest why the *soukhouan* is so critically important for understanding the Lao religious landscape. *Soukhouan* rituals thrive in contemporary Laos, refugee camps and Lao refugee communities in Europe and North America. They have been successfully adapted to meet new needs in new contexts. Their core meaning remains intact, as the contexts shift and the acts are reinterpreted. *Soukhouan* rituals are one important means of analyzing the complex relation between the different strands of the Lao religious fabric—animism, Buddhism and court Brahmanism.

*Soukhouan* rites are held to celebrate rites of passage such as marriage, pregnancy, birth and ordination; to mark the start of an undertaking such as a trip or military service; to celebrate someone's return to the community after an absence; to strengthen someone suffering from a long or serious illness; to dispel bad luck; and to welcome officials or guests to a community or a celebration (cf. LeBar and Suddard; Ngaosyvathn 1990 ;Tambiah 1970).

In contemporary Laos, *soukhouan* ceremonies still form the basis of wedding ceremonies, along with an authorization from the ministry for the marriage of its cadre (Ngaosyvathn 1989:15). Stuart-Fox notes that *soukhouan* persist in the new regime as ceremonies of welcome or farewell for guests, to make an auspicious occasion or to prepare for an important event (Stuart-Fox 1986:168). Lao refugees leaving camps to be repatriated in Laos are given a *soukhouan* ceremony to wish them luck on their return to Laos. Although some of the more magical or feudalistic language may be altered for officials, *soukhouan* rituals are not described as needing to be purged from Lao culture. That is, they are not seen as superstitious, feudalistic remnants but as an expression of egalitarian reciprocity and generosity. In fact, Ngaosyvathn sees *soukhouan* as strengthening the moral stance of the new regime by emphasizing marital fidelity and the respect of children toward their parents. Less ostentatious and expensive ceremonies also enhance the equality-oriented policy of the new government (Ngaosyvathn 1989:15). Rajah, however, argues that this image of the *soukhouan* ceremony reflects a romanticized, idealized view (Rajah 1990:313).

*Soukhouan* ceremonies vary in complexity, with weddings and the New Year occasioning the most elaborate rituals. The basic *soukhouan* structure includes a set of actions, objects and words that accomplish a ritual task. That task is to strengthen an individual's morale by attracting and binding the wandering souls firmly into the individual's body.

In the more elaborate *baci* rituals, the *khouan* are attracted back to the body by the beauty of the words and by the flowers and offerings built up on a tree-like structure from a tray or an offering bowl. Here the talent, wealth and imagination of the sponsors of the ritual can be fully displayed. The form of the offering structure differs from that in Laos, where it was usually made from banana stalks. Lao refugees from New England comment on constructing *baci*:

Here in America we make the floral offerings with leaves and flowers that we gather. At home in Laos we used to arrange the flowers differently, just the buds in rows, stuck into a banana stalk. Here we don't have banana stalks so we do it this way now....We arrange flowers in a beautiful silver bowl. On the leaves are many strings to bless our loved ones. You tie a string around the person's wrist and say a blessing for strength, health, and long life. There are different blessings for different people. When your wrists are tied in the *baci* ceremony you must keep the strings on for three days and nights. (Halpern and Pettengill 1987)

Precut lengths of white string are draped from the branches of the *baci*. The structure is decorated with fresh flowers. Beneath the *baci* are dishes of rice, boiled eggs, bananas and other fruit, alcohol and delicacies to attract a wandering soul. In North America, these delicacies include cans of Coca Cola, Twinkies and Oreo cookies. Some of the offerings are to propitiate the spirits and deities who are invited to attend the celebration.

The officiant is not a monk but a lay elder who probably spent some time in the monkhood. He is referred to as a *mau khouan* doctor and is in many ways analogous to a Brahman (cf. P. Van Esterik 1973). While relatives and friends surround the candidate to be honored around the central offering (*baci*), the officiant takes a few threads and recites prayers to attract the wandering souls back into the body of the candidate. These prayers include the Pali verses honoring the Buddha, *dhamma* and *Sangha*, the invitation to the deities (*anchern thewada*) and other prayers appropriate to the ritual context.

Following these invocations, the cotton threads are carefully picked off the *baci* and used to bind the wrist of the officiant, the celebrant and others participating in the *soukhouan*. While the elders tie string around the wrist of the celebrant, they recite a formulaic wish for the candidate, offering wishes for long life, wealth, happiness and the success of the current undertaking—ordination to the monkhood, a journey overseas, marriage, school exams. Following the *soukhouan* and the ceremony of which it forms a part, such as the ordination of a new monk, participants share a festive meal.

*Soukhouan* may also be performed in much less elaborate settings, as, for example, when a young man who finds he must suddenly leave his village goes to his elderly relatives for their blessing and good wishes for his safety and success. But he still carries with him the strings on his wrist for at least three days and nights to remind him of the strength of his family's concern and to boost his morale.

### New Year Celebrations

These celebrations, centered around the sacred Buddha image (the Prabang), were held in April in the old royal capital of Laos, Luang Prabang, and in every community throughout the kingdom at the end of the dry season. The New Year ceremonies (Songkran) were a time of purification and regeneration. Their ritual form differed among the various localities in Laos (cf. Archaimbault 1971).

In rural communities, Songkran celebrations were spread over three days of merit making and celebrations. In Toronto, the celebrations took two forms: a community festival before there was a resident monk in Toronto and a Buddhist merit-making ritual when a monk was available.

In the gym of a downtown school, about four hundred Lao gathered to celebrate the arrival of Buddhist Era 2528 (1985). Behind the rows of metal chairs were tables laden with Lao desserts, coffee and tea available at no charge. Tables of musical instruments, weaving, clothing and handmade household craft items displayed valued Lao products. While a few foreigners admired the exotic objects, many Lao children examined the same objects as exotica since, for many of them, they had never seen them in use, or participated in their production. Posters of key sites in Laos, particularly the old royal palaces of Luang Prabang and the That Luang stupa near Vientiane, and ornamental weavings decorated the walls. A large mat in the center of the floor held a flower tree hung with white strings (*baci*) and ritual objects necessary to conduct a *soukhouan* (calling the soul) ritual. On the stage, a large sign in Lao welcomed the guests and the New Year. The men wore two-or three-piece suits, the women, the magnificent silk Lao skirts with vertical stripes and a horizontal band along the lower edge, with matching scarves draped across their shoulders. The household wealth was displayed in elaborate gold jewelry (belt, pendant, pin, hair ornament and earrings) smuggled in from Laos and protected through years of harsh conditions in refugee camps (or purchased from contacts in Bangkok after the family was established in Toronto). Children who were participating in the cultural performances wore Lao dress, while others wore jeans or western-style dresses.

The program consisted of refreshments, speeches in Lao by the Lao Association of Ontario and the Lao Buddhist Association with very brief English translations, a movie on the Ban Vinai refugee camp, a performance of Lao dancing and a blessing ceremony (*soukhouan*).

The *soukhouan* ritual figures predominately in a wide range of Lao rites of passage, such as ordinations and marriage, and in community celebrations. It is most important and formal for occasions such as the New Year. The *phakhouan* or *baci*, a tree-like structure built up from an offering tray, is the central ritual item. Its form in North America differs from that in Laos where it was made from banana stalks. Here, it is often formed from wire arranged with flowers.

Under the *baci* were bowls of holy water, uncooked rice, hard-boiled eggs and cans of Coca Cola. Precut lengths of white stringwere draped from the branches. The ritual practitioner (*mau phon*, *mau khouan*) wore a blue silk *jungkhaben* (draped pants), a white tailored jacket and a silk sash. The few foreigners at the celebration rushed up to the mat to participate in the ceremony, along with a few children and old women, but most of the guests ignored the traditional blessing ceremony taking place in the center of the room. As the practitioner intoned the Pali verses—*namo tassa* (honoring the Buddha), *anchern thewada* (inviting the deities)—and a number of Lao prayers, the old women tied the strings around the wrists of the young people, wishing them good luck and prosperity in the New Year. Following this, a number of men surrounded the practitioner and exchanged blessings and strings in a much more intense and serious manner, cementing political and social ties that could affect community integration over the next year.

By the next New Year celebration, the Lao community had a resident monk, and Lao came from a number of surrounding communities to celebrate in Toronto. The celebration followed the regular Buddhist morning service. But for a tall, lanky Lao teenager in an elaborate "punk" hairdo, the regular service where laity request the Buddhist refuges (*namo tassa*) and the precepts was totally foreign to him. "My parents told me to come. I don't know what is happening," he said in English, as elders put food in his hands to present to the monks.

In Laos, the New Year is celebrated with water, a precious commodity in the hottest season in April. Water honors elderly relatives, monks and Buddha images and flows over courting couples and children in blessed relief from the hot, dry weather. A cold, wet Toronto April provides a much different setting. Following the service, as a young man who led the laity in Pali chants raised his head from paying respects to the monk, two old women cackling with glee crept up behind him and poured water and ice down his shirt.

According to the survey, 71.9 percent of the respondents celebrate April's the New Year celebrations. Most of them join the celebrations in Toronto.

### Boun  Wisaka (Vesak)

In Laos, the day of the birth, enlightenment and death of the Buddha is celebrated on a full moon day in May. Boun Wisaka falls during the period of preparing the rice fields for the new harvest before the monsoon rains banish the hot dry season in May. The Lao in Southeast Asia do not stress this opportunity for merit making, occurring as it does at the time of intensive agricultural work. What are stressed are the local celebrations, *bun bang fai* (the rocket festival), temple fairs and what observers called a "licentious" pre-Buddhist fertility rite (HRAF 1960:57).

Vesak as a Buddhist ceremony was not elaborated in Laos but was instead associated with locality spirits and jubilant fertility festivities. It is hard to imagine any Lao celebration that would be more difficult to adapt to a North American context. More recently, the LPDR actively discouraged "licentious and superstitious" festivals associated with Vesak. But to rural Lao, the most significant celebrations of this season surrounded locality guardian spirits and deities of the soil.

Ironically, Vesak is the one ritual in the Buddhist seasonal calendar that has been separated out for elaboration in North America. Freed from its place in the seasonal cycle of agricultural activities and from its strong associations with indigenous guardian spirits of fertility, it has an essential clarity of purpose that can be called upon to build a ritual of universal Buddhist appeal. While Theravada Buddhists celebrate the birth, enlightenment and *parinirvana* of the Buddha on the same day, these events fall on different days in the Mahayana ritual cycle. In North America, attempts at bringing together different Buddhist groups usually occur on weekends. Thus, the time of the Vesak celebration is flexible. A more extensive discussion of Vesak as a ritual celebrated jointly by a number of Theravada and Mahayana groups follows in the chapter on relations between different Buddhist groups.

### Rituals of the Rains Retreat

The beginning and end of the Buddhist rains retreat (Khao Phansa, Ok Phansa, Pali: *Vassa*) is only celebrated in communities with resident monks. This time period, from July to October, coincides with the period in the Lao agricultural cycle when the transplanting of rice is completed and farmers observe the critical growing period, dependent on the monsoon rains. In Toronto, it coincides with school holidays and summer vacations.

In North America, the retreat is a time of potential conflict between Lao communities. During Phansa, monks are expected to remain in their residences, reduce outside traveling and concentrate on the *dhamma* (teachings). During this period, monks are admonished not to quarrel and to behave so as to ensure harmony in the temple community (Wells 1960:164). But when there are so few monks in the country, each community competes to have one or more monks in residence for the retreat season. In 1985, the Lao community was not able to celebrate Khao Phansa because they did not have time to prepare for the occasion. The monk from Montreal who agreed to spend Phansa in Toronto only arrived the day before the Lenten period began.

With a monk in residence, September and October are times for more intensive merit making. In September and October 1985, two merit-making occasions were scheduled:

Boun Haw Khao Padabdin and Boun Haw Khao Slark. In Laos, these rituals are part of the intensification of merit-making activity during the rains retreat, coinciding with the slack agricultural season when the rice is growing. Boun Haw Khao Padabdin took place in Laos on the fifteenth day of the waning moon in the ninth month. In Toronto, September is a month of renewing social contacts and beginning a new school year. Boun Haw Khao Padabdin and Boun Haw Khao Slark are occasions for making merit for deceased relatives. At the mid-year point of the old calendar, deceased family members can visit their communities and benefit from the merit making of their relatives. Boun Haw Khao Padabdin refers to a Buddhist "commandment" to honor the dead with gifts, prayers and thoughts (HRAF 1960:57).

In 1985, Boun Haw Khao Padabdin was celebrated in late September in the underground community hall in a complex of public housing apartments. By 9:00 A.M. the hall was filled with about 350 Lao from Toronto, Hamilton, Brampton and other southern Ontario towns. The floor was covered with Lao mats with a raised platform for the monks and the altar. A large set of loudspeakers framed the platform. To the left of the altar were tables displaying nine silver and gold *kalaprapruk* (Pali: *kapparukkha*) trees decorated with bank notes. These "wishing trees" represent the leaves of the sacred Bodhi tree, according to the Wat Lao committee.

Members of the Lao Buddhist Association explained that one monk from Montreal had accepted Toronto's invitation to spend Phansa in the newly registered Wat Lao of Ontario. Three additional monks came from Montreal to celebrate the occasion. Before the ritual began, the highest-ranking monk explained the background of Boun Haw Khao Padabdin, explaining its history and meaning before the regular morning service began. Following the chanting and presentation of food, the monks transferred the merit accrued to the deceased ancestors.

Following more announcements about the newly established Wat Lao, the highest-ranking monk read a sermon about this particular merit-making occasion. In the story, a prince asks the Buddha about the benefits of merit making on this occasion. The givers would be free of danger and gain happiness, their relatives and other beings would gain shelter, and merit would be shared with other relatives. According to the words of the Buddha, "Anyone who performs charitable deeds on the ancestors day shall attain the Three Blessings: the terrestrial Blessing of being born a king, the celestial Blessing of becoming Indra, and the supreme Blessing of attaining Nirvana" (de Berval 1959:284). The monk explained that *padab* meant to decorate in a pleasing manner, to make pure and clean and to adorn with flowers of different shades and scents. *Din* he linked to the canonical interpretation that humans, composed of the four elements of earth, water, wind and fire, are composed primarily of *din* or earth. *Din* also refers to earth, the environment we share, that must be well taken care of to be productive and increase in value. *Padabdin*, then, refers to adorning humans with decorations of the body and "soul." Decorations to the "soul" are charity (Pali: *dana*), morality (Pali: *sila*) and wisdom (Pali: *bhavana*). When humans are adorned with these virtues, they are considered civilized, intelligent persons and will become widely known for their good deeds. These deeds will bring material happiness of mind in this life and the next, and the merit will also flow to the deceased.

The *kalaprapruk* trees were presented to the monks following a lively clockwise procession three times around the hall accompanied by dancing, drumming and singing (or more accurately, shouting). The nine trees came from formal groups such as the Lao Association of Hamilton, the United Front for the Protection of Laos and the National Liberation and Neutrality Movement of Laos, as well as groups of neighbors in the same apartment complex and individual families.

Boun Haw Khao Slark, usually held in the tenth lunar month, is the next major opportunity for communal merit making in the Lenten season. With the monk from Montreal still in residence, Boun Haw Khao Slark was celebrated two weeks later in the same community hall with about two hundred in attendance.

The Wat Lao committee explained that in the past, the offerings prepared for the monks were awarded to them by lottery. In North America, this has no meaning; it would be meaningless for two hundred people to assign offerings to two monks by lottery. Among the survey respondents, 81.3 percent of the sample had attended a Boun Haw Khao Padabdin ritual in Canada. This estimate may be high because the ritual was held only a few weeks before the survey was made; 74.8 percent of respondents said that they had attended a Boun Haw Khao Slark ritual in Canada.

Ok Phansa, the official end of the rains retreat, has been celebrated in Canada since 1985. In 1985 it was celebrated on Sunday, October 27, in a community center near Wat Lao. About two hundred Lao from Toronto, Hamilton, St. Catharines, Windsor, Cambridge and Stratford arrived for the occasion. Two new white, seven-tiered umbrellas sat near the Buddha image on the altar platform.

Seven *kalaprapruk* trees hung with one-and two-dollar bills were presented by groups from the visiting communities. The joy and pleasure in giving was infectious, as the trees were paraded around the hall accompanied by dancing, drums and more "shouting." When the trees were presented to the monks, sacred thread (*saisin*) encircled all trees and the monks. The thread remained in place as the monk gave a sermon about Ok Phansa, with frequent reference to situating the ritual in Toronto and Canada. Following the sermon, a dozen men and a few women posed for photographs with the trees, recording one of the rare occasions for communal merit making for families living some distance from Toronto.

In 1988, Ok Phansa was celebrated in the same community hall on October 30. In Laos, it would take place at the full moon of the eleventh month. At least three hundred people were present. An older monk from Montreal had agreed to reside in Toronto and was joined by two monks visiting from Rockford, Illinois. A local family had brought the monks to Toronto for a household merit-making ritual.

As usual, women arranged the food for the monks on rattan trays in the kitchen, while men chatted in preparation for the beginning of the service. A low stage accommodated the monks and Buddha image. About twenty men chose to sit on the stage in front of the monks with their backs to the rest of the laity, an innovation from former services. Then the regular *wan sin* was conducted.

Throughout the rains retreat, women prepare special candles. The monks chant and light the candles over water, returning the water to the layperson following the ritual act. Those unable to attend the service pass their candles to be blessed by the monks to someone who is attending the service. The holy water is then returned to them and they wash in it to purify themselves and thus participate at a distance in the communal merit making.

A special sermon was read to mark the end of the rains retreat. On this occasion, *kruat nam* (the sharing of merit through water pouring) was performed twice—once to share the merit following the presentation of food to the monks, and once following the sermon. In this way, deceased relatives and all sentient beings share merit derived from both *dana* (giving) and *bhavana* (wisdom).

### Presenting Robes

Within a month after the end of Buddhist Lent, *Kathin* celebrations are usually held to present new robes and other necessities to the monks. Each monastery receives only one *Kathin* a year. Canonically, the gift is made to a monastery and a chapter of monks. According to the Lao monks in Toronto, there has never been a *Kathin* ceremony in Canada because there must be at least five monks in residence through the Lenten period. However, 14 percent of the respondents said that they had attended a *Kathin* in Toronto. Some respondents may have been thinking of *Kathin* in Laos. Others may have contributed to *Kathin* held in another North American city or in Thailand.

*Thot phapa*, donation of "forest robes," is another ritual format for presenting new robes to monks after the *Kathin*. Robes may be presented on the branches of a wishing tree to carry out the forest theme. Only 15.9 percent of the survey respondents indicated that they had participated in a *thot phapa* ritual since coming to Canada. There is potential for confusion here, since *thot phapa* can be "tacked on" to other festivities more easily than can *Kathin*. Informants suggested that in Canada, donations on a *Kalaprapruk* tree substituted for *thot phapa*. In North America, it is money to support the temple that is always in short supply; few monks mean that fewer robes are needed compared to the need for monks' robes in Laos.

### That Luang

That Luang, celebrated in late November or early December around the stupa (reliquary) outside of Vientiane, has been described as "the most important occasion in the Lao religious calendar" (Gunn 1982:84). More so than most Lao rituals, That Luang celebrates a place as well as an event. Since the ritual of That Luang is so intimately connected with the stupa of That Luang, it is surprising that it has been transferred to North America so successfully. In Laos, government officials used to pledge allegiance to the Lao king during That Luang rituals.

The stupa housing Buddha relics was built around 1567 when the Lao capital was shifted to Vientiane. The French restored the monument after its burning in the 1870s. It has since become an important pilgrimage center. The ritual of That Luang was secularized during the revolution and served as a central rallying ground for official post liberation rallies in 1975. Its symbolic importance was further exploited when LPDR officials offered food and robes to the resident monks in 1979. Lao male refugees recognized this new role when they spoke of the celebration as more like a trade fair now, "like the Canadian National Exhibition." Without the king, the ritual is a "national ceremony" in Laos as well as in Canada. In Toronto, 64.5 percent of the survey respondents said that they had celebrated That Luang since coming to Canada.

That Luang was first celebrated in Toronto as a Buddhist merit-making occasion in 1987. On November 27, 1988, a second celebration was held. Dominating the basement community hall was a model of the stupa at Vientiane built out of bright yellow painted styrofoam. The model, standing about eight feet high, was decorated with Christmas tree lights and flowers. The model stood in the middle of the hall with the laity sitting on all sides of the model, facing the monks on the stage at the front of the room. Over 300 people attended from all over southern Ontario. According to the Lao, the stupa had been even more beautiful the year before.

The merit-making service was chanted by the resident Toronto monk (recently from Montreal), the visiting Winnipeg monk (recently from Toronto) and a visiting Lao monk from Thailand. The ceremony was elevated in importance by a visitor from Paris, a former Lao government minister. He was obviously highly respected and well known to the community. Many families claimed to be his relatives, and others spoke generally about having worked for him. He might well represent a patron of patrons, a very influential man, a nexus of influence and prestige with patron-client networks in Canada, the United States and France.

He sat on a chair at the side of the hall near the stage, wearing a three-piece suit and Lao shoulder cloth. As the hall slowly filled, he described the efforts of the current Lao government to destroy Buddhism but spoke confidently of the efforts of Lao in Laos and overseas to keep their religion alive. "They cannot stop the Lao from believing," he said with genuine admiration for the celebration in progress. Throughout the morning, members of the community came up singly and in family groups to pass on their greetings, recall shared experiences and ask about the location of family and friends.

The service progressed through the opening chants, refuges, requesting precepts and offering food. The guest was invited to come up on stage, hand the food trays to the monk and accept the blessing from the monks for the gift of food. Announcements were made while the monks ate, in addition to a short speech by the honored guest from Paris encouraging the Toronto Lao to preserve their religious traditions.

Following their meal and final chants, the three monks came to the front of the stage, while the community shifted mats and baskets to clear a space for a procession around the model of That Luang. The procession formed behind the four money trees (*kalaprapruk*), to the accompaniment of drums and cymbals, with the guest and important male community leaders leading the procession in three clockwise circumambulations of the stupa. As the procession passed the monks on the stage, the monks sprinkled holy water on the crowd. The demeanor of the chanting monks and the sedate marcher—eyes downcast and hands folded in front of chests—contrasted strikingly with the joyous singing and dancing of the middle-aged women who broke out of the throng to dance, "shout," sing and entice participation from embarrassed teenaged males sitting on the periphery of the room smirking or trying to ignore the antics of their mothers and aunts. "You would think they were drunk," muttered one black leather-jacketed youth in English. In the midst of this procession, combining both prayerful circumambulation and blessings, with raucous parade in every circuit, a handful of old women sat and prayed close to the model of the stupa, oblivious to the surrounding spectacle.

After three circuits, the worshippers placed flowers, incense and candles in flowerpots around the stupa and sat facing the stupa on all sides. Two laymen who earlier sat near the monks on the stage came down to ground level and prayed facing the stupa, while the monks returned to their seats at the back of the stage. The monk read a sermon from his book (interrupting his chanting to complain that he could not see any more without his glasses). Following the sermon, a number of dollar bills were taken from each tree, added to the collection of bills in a silver bowl and presented to the monks.

### Individual Merit Making

When monks are in residence at Wat Lao, they are available to perform services held in the homes of the Lao. They are most often invited to celebrate the occasion of a new house, an anniversary, birthday or wedding or to remove bad luck from a household.

Lao families can borrow the equipment necessary to sponsor a ritual at home from Wat Lao, if they do not have enough mats or serving trays, for example. Merit making at one house may serve several purposes—to make merit for the guests, to bless a new home and to honor deceased relatives, as at one merit-making ceremony held in an apartment near Wat Lao in September 1985.

About twenty middle-aged Lao women sat chatting on the floor of the tiny living room. The furniture had been shifted into the bedroom where the children sat watching television. Near the seat for the monk stood a small Buddha image, candles and a *kalaprapruk* tree decorated with one-and two-dollar bills. While the host family set out special foods for the monk, other families placed money and food into his begging bowl. The monk chanted the regular morning prayers and made holy water using a very special memorial candle made from six intertwined candles representing each member of the host family. The candle lengths were calculated based on the distances from the end of the fingers to inside the elbow, and from the "neck bone" to the navel and on the circumference of the head. Thus, the sets of candles were personalized representations of the sponsors of the merit-making ceremony. The candles were twisted together with the tallest one lit to drip into the bowl of holy water being made through the power of the chants.

Although a few members of the temple committee accompanied the monk to the apartment and led the chants, the occasion was primarily for women. They discussed the authenticity of the Lao food they prepared and instructed the younger women (and the anthropologist) how to make merit properly. "You must give two flowers and two candles, not one, and then you will be beautiful in your next life," explained the hostess.

The ritual also celebrated the donation of $500, payable to a temple on the border between Laos and Thailand at Nong Khai, for the purchase of a copy of the Buddhist scriptures and a receptacle for the books. The donor had been depressed and had "faced unfortunate circumstances" recently. This act of merit making would, perhaps, alter her fortune. She accepted donations from friends and family who then shared in the merit from the donation.

This form of ritual giving was popular among the Lao survey respondents: 67.2 percent had attended a household merit-making ritual in Toronto or nearby since coming to Canada.

A comparable ritual in a Thai household will be discussed later. Briefly, the important contrasts between the Lao and Thai rituals concern the bringing in of a special Thai monk experienced in international travel and seeking followers, and the fact that the guests were asked to wear white for the Thai ritual. This ritual, held in a much more expensive suburban house, was also focused around merit making, donations and special blessings, but the emphasis and mood were quite distinct from the same ritual performed in the Lao home.

In addition to the more formal memorial services organized by family members one hundred days following a relative's death, individuals can make merit at Wat Lao on the anniversary of a relative's death. A young Thai woman honored the tenth anniversary of her mother's death by providing a meal for the monks at Wat Lao. Following the blessing whereby she would receive the merit for her act, a member of the Wat Lao committee quietly directed her in the ritual words and actions necessary to transfer the merit to her mother. He wrote her mother's name on paper, and the monk burned the name over holy water. After that, the water and paper ashes were passed to her in a small plastic container. Had she been in Thailand or Laos, the ritual would have been conducted with other family members. In that context, older family members would direct younger family members who would not be expected to know the ritual procedure.

### Ordaining New Monks

To develop Lao Buddhism in North America, it must be possible to ordain novices and monks according to an authorized ordination tradition. This, for the Lao in North America, has been exceedingly difficult. From the problems in the refugee camps in Thailand to the disputes with neighbors in the cities of North America, the obstacles are incredible and widely shared from Washington to Montreal. These include the problems of finding a senior monk who can act as preceptor and has the authority to ordain (Pali: *upajjhaya*) and arranging one or two monks to act as ritual teachers. The ordination must be carried out in an ordination hall with boundary stones (Pali: *sima*); if there is no ordination hall, the ritual can take place on a consecrated raft over water. Water ordinations occur in different Theravadin traditions and are referred to in the canonical literature (Griswold and Na Nagara 1974; Ratannapanna 1968). A minimum of five monks is necessary for a valid ordination. Any mistakes in the ordination ritual invalidates the ordination. The cost of an ordination can be extremely high. And finally, there is no certainty that the ordination will be viewed as fully authentic and appropriately registered. Ordinations in Theravada Buddhism take place according to ordination traditions or lineages. Failure to be recognized as a part of an established tradition could have devastating effects on Lao Buddhism in North America. On the other hand, it is possible that Lao Buddhists may be in the process of defining a new tradition, unrecognized by the Sangha in Laos or the Thai Sangha with ecclesiastical jurisdiction in the camps.

In spite of all these problems, in May 1987, the first young Lao men were ordained as novices and then as monks in a ritual built from scriptural authority and traditional practice but modified to meet the circumstances of refugees living in Toronto. The five men were sponsored by relatives and friends, with substantial financial support from the Lao community. The four men in their twenties were ordained for the first time, while one older man (aged thirty-nine) had been ordained several times before. All five men ordained to make merit for themselves and for their mothers. Because of their work obligations, they were only able to stay in the monkhood for one week. According to Lao women, ordination even for a week makes the young men much more attractive as potential spouses. Men who are good to their mothers will be good to their wives. Since they are interested in religion, they are considered good moral men who will have a trouble-free life. As in Laos, the preordination and ordination celebrations have a particular appeal for young unmarried women. For this ordination, the preceptor and his colleague came from California, while two additional monks came from Montreal.

On the day of ordination, the community hall was filled to overflowing and decorated with special offerings related to the ordination ceremony. These offering structures (*khong uppasombot*) contained the requisites of a monk (including robes, bowl, umbrella, slippers and razor) in addition to bedding, items of personal use and a "wishing tree" (*kalaprapruk*) decorated with dollar bills. These gifts were presented to the temple for the use of the five new monks.

At the early morning preordination service, the candidates wore white and already had their heads shaved. The monks began the service by paying respects to the Triple Gem and giving the precepts. As the monks continued their chants, the guests placed food in the monks' bowls. This was followed by the candidates' giving the food to the *Sangha*. Ordinarily the monks accepted the food and blessed the laity after they ate. Because of the time constraints, the blessing was made before the monks ate, with the result that the monks and laity ate at approximately the same time.

Meanwhile, the candidates moved over to a special structure, the *baci* draped with white strings, to conduct a very important ritual called in Thai *tham khwan nak*, calling the candidates' souls. The *soukhouan nak* rituals are an important part of Lao ordinations, and the basic structure of a *soukhouan* ritual has already been described. This ritual refers to the novice as a *nak* (Pali: *naga*), a serpent who assumed human shape and was ordained as a monk only to be expelled by the Buddha when he was revealed not to be human. On leaving the Sangha, he asked that candidates to the monkhood be called *nak* in his memory, and this wish was granted. The ritual, performed by a ritual specialist brought from Montreal (*mau khouan*), strengthens the novices and prepares them for their new status. For lack of time, the ritual specialist had to condense the usual long chants calling the souls of the *naks* and directed the relatives and sponsors to give their individual blessings to the *naks* by tying the sacred threads around their wrists. The *soukhouan nak* reminds the candidates that the merit they make by ordaining should be transferred to their mothers and sponsors.

The condensation necessary to complete each step in the ritual at the community hall was necessary because about two hundred people had to make their way to the harborfront of a busy city to board a charter boat in short order. Each sponsor group chose about fifty persons as guests at the ordination on board the large charter boat. Normally, there would be a procession led by musicians to lead the *nak* to the place of ordination. Because of the crowd at the waterfront and the fact that the charter boat was rented by the hour, the parade was dispensed with and guests followed the monks and *nak* directly onto the boat.

The ordination took place in a small cabin on the upper deck after the boat was cruising on the lake. The steps of the ordination service were carefully followed, for the purity of the ordination ritual is a key component in the legitimation of the *Sangha*. This is of particular concern for Buddhists in North America who want to be linked to an authorized ordination tradition.

There are numerous sources on the procedure for ordination in the Theravada tradition, and the ritual details will not be described here. The steps include obtaining the consent of the sponsors for the ordination, changing from white to yellow robes and requesting the ten precepts from the senior monk. At this point, the *nak* became novices. Next, the two monks who acted as mentors asked a set of questions to determine eligibility for higher ordination. These qualifications included whether the *nak* is a male human being of the correct age, with consent of parents or spouse, is free of debt and disease and is not a fugitive. Following an additional set of chants and responses, the new novices became new monks. Their first act was to transfer merit to their parents and sponsors. After each *nak* completed the ritual, the preceptor lectured the new monks on the rules of the order and the behavior expected of new monks. Following the ordination, the new monks joined the guests for photographs and conversation.

The final stage of the ritual took place back in the community hall near the Wat Lao. Here the ritual practitioner (*mau khouan*) led the remaining guests in formally presenting the gifts to the temple for the use of the new monks. All participants shared in this meritorious act by being encircled by a sacred thread by the monks as they chanted. As a final act, the merit accrued by this act was immediately shared with all sentient beings, particularly deceased relatives. The service ended with the leading monk blessing the crowd by sprinkling holy water on them to drive away evil and bring good luck.

The ordination in Toronto marked the height of the commitment by the Lao community to reestablishing their Buddhist institutions in Canada. The brief time the new monks spent in the monkhood was irrelevant to the cost of the ritual. Even three-day ordinations require the same massing of financial, human and material resources, and require knowledge of the total ritual sequence on the part of all participants. During this ordination, members of the sponsoring group were able to prompt the *nak* when their memories lapsed. How long the knowledge of ritual procedures will remain in the heads of the laity when ordinations occur so infrequently in North America remains to be seen.

The financial resources necessary to conduct a proper ordination are considerable. The boat charter alone cost more than $1,000. The sponsors raised funds through donations from friends and relatives. Wat Lao did not request funds from government agencies, nor did they want to request too many donations from the Lao community lest they cause bad feelings and envy among Lao Christians.

Among the Lao informants, 48.5 percent had been to a monk's ordination since coming to Canada, and 25.2 percent had been to a novice's ordination. Most informants were probably referring to the Toronto ordination described above. However, the responses are ambiguous because the candidate is first ordained as a novice and then ordained as a monk by additional ritual steps. .Respondents may have been referring to the first half of the service of ordination for a monk when they reported having attended a novice's ordination.

### Thera Piset, Special Monk

In May 1989, the elderly monk from Montreal currently residing in Wat Lao was honored by the Lao community around Toronto with a ceremony called *Thera piset*, to identify him as a special monk. This ceremony was initiated by the laity (Pali: *upasaka*, laymen; *upasika*, laywomen) and upgrades the title of the monk. As one member of the Lao Buddhist Association explained, it was arranged to honor the monk and to keep him happy in Toronto. With no precedent for conducting this ceremony in Toronto, the association turned to an experienced layman in Montreal who told them what to purchase and how to prepare for the ritual event. He also came with the two Lao monks from Montreal and led the laity through the ritual performance (with a few hesitations and false starts, but no one knew how to prompt or help him through the long recitations). The community went to a great deal of trouble and expense to arrange an authentic ritual event. Although the weather outside the community hall was hot and oppressive, the frigid air-conditioning in the basement hall made the water-pouring honoring the elderly monk a chilly affair.

The service began with the regular *wan sin* chants by the Toronto monk with two visiting monks from Montreal, one visiting monk from Rochester, two Khmer monks from Toronto and a Lao novice who had been ordained the evening before in Wat Lao. He planned to remain a monk for seven days and had planned his stay to precede his upcoming marriage. Since he was twenty-three, he could be ordained as a monk, not a novice. But the family and community did not have funds to cover the costs of a water ordination, and he had to settle for ordination as a novice. Unlike other Lao services in Toronto, for this service about eight men dressed in white and took the eight precepts. By this act of devotion, they agreed to keep three more precepts than the general laity, including fasting after the noon meal.

A large decorated bed and a long serpent constructed of wood decorated the normally austere hall. The bed, with a canopy, sat in the middle of the room. On it were arranged gifts from the temple committee and the laity, including new robes, a new begging bowl, a rice steamer, pots, a lamp, sheets, towels, flowers, triangular and rectangular cushions and a set of foil cones used for *soukhouan* rituals.

Following the presentation of food, flowers, incense and money to the monks, the monks chanted a special blessing for deceased relatives. The laity who wished to transfer merit to their deceased relatives here or in Laos wrote their relatives' names on a sheet of paper. The monks burned the names over a bowl of water using a special candle. All the gifts to the monk were encircled with a sacred thread held by the monks. By the power of the chanting, the morality of the monks and laity and the intentions to give with an open heart, the moral community in Toronto shared the merit gained with their named relatives and with all sentient beings. This act was completed by *kruat nam*, where the laity poured small bottles of water into silver bowls, while the monks chanted. Although most families used simple household bottles and hammered aluminum and silver-plated bowls from Laos, one man used an exquisite six-inch-high carved silver vase, probably an heirloom cherished and protected through flight, refugee camp and resettlement.

In preparation for the bathing ceremony, the monk to be honored and another senior Khmer monk were carried on small tables in a procession led by the monks around the hall three times to the accompaniment of music, gongs and "shouts." The attention then focused on the carved, wooden serpent (*naga*) with a hollow trough in the center. The *naga* was suspended from the ceiling on one side of the room, with the head tipped down. Beneath the *naga's* mouth the elderly monk sat in a small plastic wading pool. The men who were keeping the eight precepts approached the tail of the *naga*, poured water into the central cavity that flowed into the *naga's* mouth, then into a cotton bag suspended from the mouth, and onto the head and shoulders of the elderly monk. Another senior monk accompanied the monk receiving the water blessing to dress him in new dry robes received from the laity at the end of the ceremony. While the men were pouring water, a woman near the *naga* asked, "can the women pour water?" On receiving an affirmative answer, dozens of women rushed up to the wooden structure and, using the water they had previously used for *kruat nam* or water in a nearby pail, one at a time they poured water down the trough in the *naga* and onto the monk. Meanwhile, a lay leader in white hit a large gong.

On a presentation tray near the monk, two silver strips and one gold strip with strings attached to one end awaited a ceremonial moment that passed very quickly. These objects of gold (*dap kum*) and silver (*dap nyng*) were placed around the monk's head to symbolize his change of status. The gong was then sounded three times. The objects were designed and made by a Toronto jeweler who charged $500 for making the items. The monk then received his new bowl and made a ritual circumambulation of the hall while laity paid their respects and placed bills in his new bowl. The monk then sat in front of the bed laden with gifts and accepted the donations with a prayer. Finally, the senior monk from Montreal gave a speech about the occasion of *Thera piset* and its link to basic Buddhist teachings.

## The Role of Wat Lao in the Community

Wat Lao is neither wealthy nor powerful. Its various locations in a number of high-rise, low-income apartment units were inconvenient for monks and not conducive to a contemplative life-style, to say the least. But these locations are centrally located for the Lao. Several other Lao associations are supported with government funding, but Wat Lao is not eligible for government funds. Yet in spite of the difficulties Wat Lao faces, its existence is very important to the Lao community in southern Ontario. Other communities report a similar dependence on their temple associations. In France, Condominas reports that Lao refugees build temples to reconstruct their ethnic identity in a completely different foreign environment "and find in their temples not simply a religious expression but also the warmth and satisfaction of being together from the same culture" (Condominas 1987:451).

The efforts to set up Wat Lao and the Lao Buddhist Association and the participation in rituals are occasions for doing other non-Buddhist things such as exchanging news, displaying the beauty of Lao textiles and forming patron-client alliances. For the Lao in many parts of North America, there would be few opportunities to do these other things unless appropriate religious events are celebrated. The Lao have made great efforts to recreate some aspects of their religious environment in Canada and provide opportunities for regular merit making. Between the events, individuals and families visit the resident monk at Wat Lao for a variety of reasons. As one respondent wrote, "I go when I feel like it."

In the survey, 82 percent of the respondents reported visiting the monks at Wat Lao. About half the respondents did not provide any reason for their visit, but 57 respondents provided reasons (Table 4.2).

**Table 4.2**          **Reasons for Visiting Wat Lao**

| Reason | Number of Respondents | Percentage |
|---|---|---|
| Respect Buddhism | 14 | 24.6 |
| Advice from monk | 12 | 21.1 |
| Make merit | 10 | 16.6 |
| "Family culture" | 8 | 14.0 |
| Learn, study | 7 | 12.3 |
| Pray | 3 | 5.3 |
| Can't attend services | 2 | 3.5 |
| "Feel like it" | 1 | 1.8 |
| Total | 57 | 100.0 |

The first reason stresses visiting the temple out of respect for Buddhism, because "I am a Buddhist" and because "I believe in Buddhism." I interpret this to reflect personal identity as Buddhist.

The second reason stresses meeting with the monk to chat and listening to his advice. Refugees come to the monk to talk about problems they have in adjusting to Canadian society and for advice regarding their children. For example, families with teenagers have particular problems surrounding depression, school pressures and courtship.

The third reason is solidly supported by other questions in the survey and observations made throughout the study. In fact, since several questions address directly how merit is made, the respondents may have thought that they had already discussed merit making enough. Thus, merit making may be under represented as a reason for going to Wat Lao. Reasons surrounding merit-making include receiving blessings after giving to the monks. The blessing after the intention to give with a pure heart is as important as the merit received and often takes the tangible form of holy water that can be taken home in small bottles.

The fourth reason reflects the fact that to be Lao is to be Buddhist—that the respondents grew up and were socialized within Buddhist families and Buddhist communities. Their ethnic identity was expressed in phrases such as "Buddhism is part of my family culture, part of Lao culture."

Fewer respondents reported going to Wat Lao to study or learn about Buddhism, although some mentioned the need to learn about morality. Informally, it became clear that the respondents have a great concern for their children's understanding of Buddhism. They express great fear that their children will not have an opportunity to learn about Buddhism, and they worry that they do not have the knowledge to teach their children themselves. The Lao therefore seek a monk who is skilled at teaching Buddhism.

While three informants reported going to Wat Lao to pray, two have a more practical concern. Because of their work schedule and the fact that they live outside of Toronto, they have no opportunity to attend regular *wan sin* or special ritual events. They therefore have no opportunity for communal merit making and must make merit individually at Wat Lao, a less desirable situation.

The one respondent who wrote "when I feel like it" may not have been being flippant but instead reflecting his feeling about visiting Wat Lao on the spur of the moment.

During ritual events, a great deal of money is collected for various purposes, including to support Wat Lao and the resident monk. Monks are not permitted to handle money, and their modest needs are willingly met by the temple committee or by community members. Various monks have used this donated money to provide interest-free emergency loans for community members in need. In this way, money donated at merit-making services circulates back into the Lao community in the form of an emergency insurance fund.

Among the resources that many Lao refugees bring to North America is their knowledge of Buddhism. This knowledge is reflected in the Buddhist rituals described in this chapter. While this resource may not appear to be critically important to initial adaptation of Lao to North America, it is more accurate to say that analysts have simply not examined this aspect of refugee adaptation. In the next chapter, I place Lao Buddhism in the context of other Buddhist resources.

# Chapter Five

## Brothers and Sisters in the Dhamma

**Lao Buddhism in the World Tradition**
In the last chapter, we saw the efforts of Lao refugees to retain their Buddhist heritage in Canada. From this perspective, it would be easy to overstress the isolation and ethnic particularism of Lao Buddhism. Historically Lao Buddhism was never a closed national religion. Even the palladium, the Prabang statue, had come from Sri Lanka via Angkor Wat in Cambodia. Thai monks, particularly from the Thammayut sect, regularly entered Laos until the Lao Popular Front condemned them as agents of American imperialists and Thai reactionaries (Lafont 1982:149). Thai and Lao monks regularly interacted to re-establish, purify and strengthen monastic discipline and the ordination tradition. Thus, Lao Buddhism participated in the broader Buddhist sphere of Theravada Buddhism.

In contemporary Laos, Buddhist monks participate in international Buddhist conferences such as the Asian Buddhist Conference for Peace with headquarters in Ulan Bator, Mongolia. This group pledged solidarity with brother Buddhists in Vietnam and Kampuchea (Gunn 1982:93). In fact, Lafont argues that Lao Buddhism no longer corresponds to Theravada Buddhism and is evolving toward a form of Mahayana (LaFont 1982:160). However, this speculation is unsupported by evidence on current Lao religious practice.

The tensions between ethnic particularistic Buddhism and an emerging form of international non-sectarian Buddhism are played out among the Lao refugees in North America as well. In this chapter, the practice of Lao Buddhism is framed more broadly to examine where Lao Buddhism fits within the range of Buddhist groups in Toronto. To what extent do they share similar objectives and perceptions about the new Buddhist polity emerging in North America?

**Relations with Theravada Communities**
Wat Lao in Toronto has particularly close (if not always cordial) relations with Wat Lao in Montreal. Since Montreal was the first Canadian city to have a resident Lao monk, many Toronto Lao contributed to the temple in Montreal and made

merit in person or through donations to the Montreal temple. This was the only opportunity the Lao in Toronto had to make merit after settling in their new homeland. Montreal also supplied Toronto with their first temporary and long-term monks. The two communities remain in contact through visits. For example, recently a Lao women's group formed and planned a two-day trip to Montreal arranged by the women's association there. They reciprocated with the Montreal group for a return visit to Toronto.

In spite of the difficulties some refugees face in crossing the American/Canadian border, relations between Lao in Toronto and Lao groups in Rochester, New York and Rockford, Illinois are quite close. Friends from Rochester visit the Wat Lao for special services, and a special gift exchange, *thot phapa*, was recently planned with the Buddhist Association in Rochester.

Monks from Rockford, Illinois, have officiated at a number of Toronto Lao celebrations. However, monks as a category are not well understood by immigration officials, and the Lao recount stories of problems monks face at the border. A bilingual language and cultural broker would probably have been able to solve the following problem. A monk from the United States was turned back at the border by Canadian immigration authorities because he answered that he had no money, as is expected of Theravadin monks. However, he was fully supported by lay groups on both sides of the border.

Wat Lao Buddhavong in Washington, D.C., was founded in 1977, and has made a substantial contribution to the establishment of Lao Buddhism in North America. However, because of the distance, the Lao monks from Washington have not had a great deal of contact with the Toronto community.

The refugee experience brings national and ethnic groups into new kinds of relationships with each other, as well as with the receiving nation. To North Americans, both Laos and Cambodia were the "sideshows" of the Vietnam conflict; they were, perhaps, the less progressive and less interesting colonial possessions in Indochina for the French; to the Thai, they were the "other," the "younger brother," the neighboring Buddhist states whose zeniths and nadirs directly affected Thailand's security in a world of pulsating galactic polities. These historical subjectivities are usually lost in the refugee discourse where war and disruption define the total reality of daily existence, and past and present refer to before and after 1975. In the past, Lao and Cambodians competed with each other in the realm of tribute, bride wealth, Buddhist relics and sacred images; in North America, they compete for space in government buildings, dates for celebrations and money for ethnic heritage programs.

When Southeast Asian refugees entered North America, they were numerically dominated by the Vietnamese. Thus, both lowland Lao and Khmer refugees tended to receive less individualized attention except during the publicity concerning the atrocities of the Pol Pot regime and the subsequent Cambodian famine. In Toronto, the pattern of immigration of all these groups was quite similar, with a peak in 1979 and a gradual reduction in government sponsorship of refugees throughout the 1980s.

The Lao, Khmer and Vietnamese associations funded by the secretary of state for multiculturalism used to be side by side in a downtown government building. The staffs of the three associations had to communicate with each other in French or English. The Lao and Khmer associations cooperated by scheduling community and religious events so as not to conflict with each other. Buddhist calendrical rites such as the beginning and end of the Buddhist rains retreat, Vesak and the traditional New Year ceremony are celebrated on the same day in Laos and Cambodia. In Toronto, they were scheduled on alternate weekends so that resources could be shared and the committees could attend each other's celebrations.

Before the Lao community in Montreal was able to support a resident monk, the Khmer community in Montreal offered assistance. The two Lao monks slept for several months in the Cambodian temple until their facilities were ready. In Ottawa, where there was no Lao temple, a young Lao man was ordained in the Cambodian temple. Now that Toronto has a resident Lao monk and a resident Khmer monk, the two reside in neighboring apartments in the same apartment building in the Jane-Finch area.

Lao and Khmer are not mutually intelligible languages; they belong to different language families. The monks who live side by side cannot easily communicate. They share the sacred language of the Theravada texts, Pali, but not a vernacular language. Neither monk speaks much English or French. Dumoulin argues that Khmer Buddhism modernized further and faster than Lao Buddhism because of greater Khmer contact with the Thai Sangha (Dumoulin 1976:40). Nevertheless, the Lao and Cambodian monks share a ritual tradition, and their proximity in the apartment building may encourage more cooperation. For example, in May 1989 two Khmer monks joined Lao monks from Montreal and Rochester in a ceremony to honor the elderly Lao monk and raise his monastic status (see Chapter Four, Special Monk). Condominas writes that in the temples in Paris, Lao monks are invited to ceremonies in the Khmer temple, as if from a neighboring village. "In exile, the ethnic community takes the place of the village community" (Condominas 1987:451).

There are very few signs of sectarian or ethnic pride behind the efforts of the Lao Buddhist Association to establish a version of Lao Buddhism in Toronto. The Lao simply want an opportunity to practice their religion in Canada. But occasionally, there is mention of a vision beyond the pragmatics of offering a place to make merit. To paraphrase from the sermon of a visiting monk from Montreal, "When many people come together, it gives strength and power to religion in this country, and to the dead—our parents and ancestors are happy that the religion is here in Ontario." The need to establish Theravada Buddhism in Toronto is fuelled in part by the fear that Buddhism is declining in Laos. This fear was well founded in the 1970s, but is less so now that Buddhist practice is tolerated in Laos. But the Lao did not leave their country because of religious persecution per se. Attacks on Buddhist institutions and personnel were a by-product of revolution and war, not a deliberate strategy as in Cambodia. Refugees seldom plan to leave their country and for the most part leave reluctantly to save themselves from real or perceived danger. They are less likely to be cognitively and emotionally detached from their pasts and thus are in greater need of their traditional institutions for immediate survival. Ancient rituals carry great significance for parents whose children have been born in refugee camps even if they have little meaning for the children themselves. As one parent expressed it, they need the services "so our children will know where they came from."

On the other hand, immigrants who plan to leave their home, for whatever reason, have an opportunity to detach themselves somewhat from their past identity. Their retrospective seeking for their lost roots may well be a feature of the adaptation of second-generation immigrants. Some of the difficulties between Lao and Thai coordination of Buddhist services reflect the considerable differences between immigrants and refugees.

Thai-Lao cooperation is at one level an obvious result of common heritage, language and geographical proximity. At another level, Thai-Lao relations are fraught with tensions, for the Thai in Toronto represent a small, select immigrant group of well-educated professionals, and the Lao, a large refugee population of varying backgrounds, the majority being undereducated rural farmers. Their orientation to their pasts, present conditions and futures are often diametrically opposed. For many elderly Lao, returning home may be a cherished dream; Canadian life is a brief, cold sojourn until repatriation is possible.

The sources of potential tension between Thai and Lao are great. Each carry ethnic stereotypes of the other, reinforced often for the Lao by experiences with the Thai military or with refugee camp officials in Thailand. Lao resent Thai refugee camp rules and Thai legislation regarding resettlement and repatriation. At the same time, they recognize that the Thai have extended substantial humanitarian aid as a country of first asylum for Indochinese refugees.

In many communities, the differences between Thai and Lao may be primarily class differences reinforced by basic differences between immigrants and refugees. Thai speak of the likelihood that Lao men will be drunk and disorderly at social occasions. Lao speak of the Thai as being more interested in making money than making merit.

In spite of these tensions, close relations are possible, particularly when strengthened by intermarriage. In addition, some Thai from the northeast refer to themselves as Lao and attend Lao religious and social events not as Thai but as Lao. In these cases, the ethnic category of Isan (inhabitants of northeast Thailand) permits Canadian Thai to become Lao for particular purposes. This is particularly easily accomplished if the Thai also speak Lao. However, they have never experienced refugee conditions. But as the past Thai ambassador to Canada, Manaspas Xuto, said in an informal social gathering of Thai and Lao, Thai and Lao should be in harmony, love and respect each other as brothers and sisters and help each other as friends (TAC 1985).

If members of the Thai community want to build a temple or support a permanent monk in Toronto, or any other North American city, they need the support of the Lao. A Thai monk in Los Angeles estimated that a community of 5,000 to 8,000 Thai would be necessary to support a Thai temple. Wealthy Thai households can and do bring famous monks from Thailand for brief periods of time to conduct specific services or offer brief *dhamma* or meditation courses. But the Thai community is too small to build and maintain a Theravada temple and to establish an ordination tradition. The Lao have the numbers to support a temple and ordain novices and monks but not the funds to build a temple. The Thai have a Buddha image, altar, texts and a text cabinet and funds to construct a temple. They also have clear criteria for a resident monk. According to a past member of the Thai Buddhist Association, the Thai community wants an "exemplary monk" from the Thammayut sect who can teach *dhamma* and meditation and speaks Thai, Lao and English. There has been substantial discussion over a possible temple name. Some want the temple to be identified as Thai (for example, Wat Thai); others insist it should be identified somehow as Thai *and* Lao. One compromise suggested was Thera Wat, a suggestion that augurs well for a broader appeal to other Theravada groups in Toronto. Or, as one Thai devotee suggested, "maybe we could convert some Canadians." The comment was not intended seriously, and those who overheard it at a suburban house-blessing ritual laughed gently.

One merit-making ritual held in a Thai household illustrates some of the differences between Lao and Thai approaches to Buddhist practice. My Thai research assistant and I were asked to wear white to this house-blessing ritual held on a June evening in suburban Toronto. The two Thai monks who were to officiate had agreed to come to Toronto at the request of the house owner, who heard about their visit to Chicago through a Thai friend there. The monks were truly modern-day *phra thudong* (traveling monks), as their travels included Japan, California, New York, Florida and

Washington, D.C., as well as Toronto and Chicago. The senior monk who led the chanting and did most of the speaking wore the dark brown robes and Burmese meditation beads of a *phra thudong*.

Forest monks have a long tradition in Southeast Asia. The opposition between forest dwellers (Pali: *arannavasi*) and town dwellers (Pali: *gamavasi*) is acknowledged in the Pali canon. The forest monks in Thailand generally observe a number of ascetic practices and practice meditation. According to Tambiah, they view the desirable relation between monk and layman as one of nonreciprocity—the monk's acceptance of gifts without any obligation to return (Pali: *mutta-muttaka*) (Tambiah 1984:54). On the other hand, these traveling monks may reciprocate directly to the laity through their psychic powers and capacity to sacralize images and amulets.

The *phra thudong* from Thailand followed in this tradition by chanting special verses (*katha*) so that those attending would successfully accomplish whatever tasks they undertook. After the *katha* he gave detailed scriptural references to the life of the Buddha, as if he felt it necessary to teach *dhamma* as well as provide ritual services. He then gave a second *katha* to ensure happiness within the family. This, too, was followed by stories from northern Thai historical chronicles and from the Jatakas (stories of the former lives of the Buddha). The longest part of the evening was spent in recounting his own life story, including his first encounters with spirits, his meditation experiences and details of his previous lives. Through his powers, he traveled through the worlds of ghosts, hungry ghosts (*phi pret*) and angels, seeing and describing the different levels of heavens and hells and claiming to have seen the Buddha. He also described his experiences with spirits who wished to make contact with their living relatives. The monk would locate the relatives of these spirits and pass on the spirits' messages. There was great interest in this discussion among the twenty or so assembled friends and relatives of the Thai host.

Around 10:30 P.M., laity requested and received the precepts, and the monk began *sadoh kroh*, a blessing ceremony to remove bad luck from a person or place. He said a magical formula and blew over a platter of seven kinds of fruit and then distributed the fruit. Sacred thread (*saisin*) surrounded the group assembled on the floor of the spacious living room, and children were called in to join in the blessing. A number of children received special blessings, and a *taw ayut* (a special prayer to extend the life of an older person) was conducted. Personal Buddha images and amulets were sanctified and blessed at the same time, and the senior monk distributed his photograph and picture on an amulet. The monks made a supply of holy water (*nammon*) for the household and guests and sprinkled the assembled devotees with holy water in a final blessing. Following these acts, fund raising began in earnest, both to contribute to the costs of conducting the ceremony and to contribute to the special meditation center he had built in the hills north of Chiang Mai. While it is extraordinarily risky for monks to make claims about meditation powers and spiritual journeys, it is not unknown in Thailand, and such monks may be thought to have the power to select winning lottery numbers. Rather surprising was the monks' eating ice cream after midnight, arguing that it was now morning.

This event underscores some of the difficulties that Lao refugees and Thai immigrants would have in combining their spiritual resources in a single temple. The most obvious differences are wealth and class: the luxury of a newly built and decorated suburban house with plush carpeting, modern furniture and extra bedrooms for housing visiting monks and their lay assistants, contrasted with crowded, one-bedroom apartments in dilapidated, noisy, subsidized public housing units. The Lao do not have the resources to spend on lavish ritual events as individuals, but when they pool their resources in large cooperative groups, they can produce lavish community rituals. The Thai are more likely to bring in a monk for an individual crisis or a household-based ritual, with a network of close friends and relatives invited to participate. The Lao are more likely to bring in a monk for a community-based ritual sponsored by Wat Lao or the Lao Buddhist Association. Funds for community rituals are raised through past and current merit-making contributions. Lao rituals in Toronto have generally depended on monks from Montreal, with limited opportunities for bringing monks from Rochester or Chicago. These monks are invited because they have successfully developed a Lao temple or established a tradition of authentic Buddhist seasonal rituals in their communities. They may be "village monks," but they are village monks who have successfully adapted the Lao religious tradition to a North American setting. They are respected monks; they are not sought after for their individual esoteric skills but for their representativeness of Lao community values.

The Thai, who did not have access to a resident monk to meet their regular needs during the time of research, seek out the more exceptional monks with reputations for teaching, meditation or more esoteric spiritual skills such as the capacity to communicate directly with spirits or to predict the future. There is a strong tradition in Thailand supporting monks who possess *saiyawet* or magical knowledge and practices useful for alleviating people's suffering (Tambiah 1984:267). The Lao village monks who seldom have had advanced Pali training or other educational opportunities may be unable to attract and hold the attention of Lao children and teenagers whose parents want them to study Buddhism. Only the best educated and most innovative monks could make *dhamma* classes relevant to teenagers who have few or no memories of community-based rituals in Laos. They have, instead, memories of refugee camps and of struggles to adapt to North American schools. Some do not even speak Lao and would have little reason to respect a village monk.

If the Thai can only bring in one monk occasionally, they want a "super-monk" who can offer a wide range of ritual and personal services. The Thai have great respect for the meditation masters in northeastern Thailand. While it is possible that a Lao-speaking monk from northeastern Thailand may have great skills as a meditation teacher, he is unlikely to want to establish a temple in North America and unlikely to be useful to the Lao, since he would not have shared the experience of refugee flight and camp life. The Lao monks who have an understanding of the refugee experience are desperately needed in Lao refugee camps in Thailand and may be increasingly important in repatriation programs in Laos. Thus, the Lao refugee community and the Thai immigrant community face very different problems in attracting a monk for a short-or long-term stay in Toronto.

In some ways, the Thai community need the Lao in order to develop a moral community that would feed and support a Thai-Lao monk and temple. Yet, they also recognize that they might well be swamped with Lao, and lose control of the committees determining temple policy. The Thai generally let the Lao know of their planned religious functions because they need more people to attend. Contact is made through the Lao Buddhist Association. But the leaders of the Thai Association said that the Lao rarely reciprocate because they have enough people to carry out the services themselves. Thus, even among the closest "coreligionists" there is minimal cooperation and limited interest in building Theravadin institutions that serve the needs of both communities.

A number of Lao Buddhists have attended services at the Mahavihara Sri Lankan temple located in the eastern suburbs of Toronto in a former Kentucky Fried Chicken outlet. This is probably the largest Theravadin community in Toronto and supports two Sri Lankan monks who are active both in the Sri Lankan Buddhist community and the more general Buddhist activities in Toronto. The Toronto Mahavihara has a substantial advantage over other Theravadin communities because of the English-fluency of their clergy and the amount of Buddhist materials printed in English. They put out a newsletter in English called *Toronto Buddhist* containing questions from the laity and answers from the senior monk, *dhamma* stories for children, Triple Gem puzzles for children, Pali and English translations of the Triple Gem, the refuges and the five precepts and announcements of current activities. Usually members of the Lao Buddhist Association will be invited and often attend Buddhist functions at the Mahavihara.

One interesting ritual occasion was held at the Toronto Mahavihara in October 1985 to celebrate the twenty-ninth anniversary of Dr. Ambedkar's historic conversion to Buddhism. In October 1956, Dr. Ambedkar led half a million followers in a formal declaration of adherence to Buddhism, and more conversions followed, particularly among untouchables. The Ambedkar Mission is part of the Buddhist revival movement in India that is spreading around the world with South Asian immigrants. This service celebrated the conversion and subsequent initiation of Ambedkar as a Theravada Buddhist. Since Ambedkar grew up as a Hindu, he had a formal initiation to disassociate himself from his Hindu past. The Ambedkar Mission has retained the ritual importance of conversion and initiation by marking the first time a convert recites the refuges and precepts publicly. After the Sri Lankan monk gave the precepts in Pali, an additional set of articles recited in Punjabi. Following the service, conducted in

English, Pali and Punjabi, the Lao present at the ceremony mentioned how unusual it was to have a Buddhist initiation ceremony. However, he saw the possibility that the Lao might have to develop such a service for Lao who had converted to Christianity in the camps and wished to return to practicing Buddhism, now that it was possible to do so in Toronto.

Most Lao Buddhists practice Buddhism within their own households or in community celebrations organized by Wat Lao. For many Lao, women in particular, lack of facility in English restricts their participation in ecumenical Buddhist services. Even if they were not committed to the practice of an exclusively Lao Buddhism, they would have no reason to collaborate with other Theravadin groups in Toronto such as the Burmese, Cambodian or Sri Lankan because these groups have no access to financial or other resources for the development of a generalized Theravada Buddhism. These ethnic groups share only an order of service and the sacred language of Pali. In fact, Burmese, Khmer and Lao belong to three totally unrelated language families in mainland Southeast Asia: Tibeto-Burman, Mon-Khmer and Tai-Kadai. They may share some of the same difficulties in trying to develop or maintain their version of Buddhism in a Judeo-Christian city, but they have no other basis for cooperation.

The exclusive focus on the particularistic Lao practice of Buddhism is reflected in the responses to the survey question on attendance at non-Lao Buddhist services. The group of survey respondents probably represent the Lao who are most interested in Buddhism. But among this highly committed group, only 28.9 percent had ever attended a non-Lao Buddhist service. Among those who had attended other Buddhist services, five had been to "North American Buddhist services" (quite likely Vesak or other ecumenical services organized by the Buddhist Council of Canada), four to Thai services, one person to a Sri Lankan service, and one to a Vietnamese service. The two men who reported going to several Buddhist services probably represented the Lao Buddhist Association at these ecumenical Buddhist services.

## Cooperation with Mahayana and Non-sectarian Buddhism

If Wat Lao has few reasons to collaborate with other Theravada groups, it is even less likely to be able to work successfully with local Mahayana groups. Mahayana Buddhism is a family of lineages dominant in North, Central and East Asia. Unlike Theravada Buddhism, which is basically one lineage with many sublineages, Mahayana Buddhism has several different theoretical systems or methods: Madhyamika, Yogacara and Vajrayana. The elaboration of these theoretical systems may have encouraged the derogatory image of Theravada as a less sophisticated, less "worthy" school of Buddhist thought. The differences between these two traditions can be clarified by examining their different interpretations of the Buddha, the dharma and the Sangha. "In the Theravada the Buddha is a discoverer who points out the Path, but in the Mahayana he becomes a saviour by whose grace beings can hope to be redeemed" (Rajavaramuni 1984:34). They share the same dharma, although Mahayana has developed some aspects into more complex metaphysics. The Sangha or monastic order is more central and disciplined in Theravadin communities (Dumoulin 1976:36). Blofeld suggests that Mahayana temples may seem lax because the monastic traditions were developed in colder climates "where the ancient rules pertaining to garments and hours of meals cannot be observed without damage to health" (Blofeld 1971:27). However, these doctrinal differences are not the only reason why Lao Buddhists are unlikely to be able to work with local Mahayana groups. One can easily understand Lao and Khmer hostility to the Vietnamese as one obstacle to Theravada-Mahayana cooperation in North American cities. In Toronto, in addition to Vietnamese Buddhist temples, there are several Korean, Chinese, Japanese, Tibetan and Sino-Vietnamese Buddhist temples with mostly Asian immigrant and refugee populations. There are also a number of centers where the majority of practitioners are westerners such as Dharmadhatu (Tibetan), Gaden Choling (Tibetan) and several Zen centers. It is the Mahayana groups that have pressed for more organization and recognition of a Buddhist presence in Canada. The founding of the Buddhist Council of Canada in 1979 brought together many of these groups in a loose coalition to further Buddhist interests in

Canada. Among the first of their projects was the organization of Vesak celebrations, commemorating the birth, enlightenment and death of the Buddha. The celebration illustrates some of the problems faced by groups promoting a nonsectarian form of Buddhism.

It is not by chance that Vesak was chosen as the communal ritual to celebrate in a nonsectarian Buddhist service. Many of the innovations associated with international Buddhism were introduced by the Buddhist Theosophical Society founded by ane American named Olcott in Sri Lanka in 1880. He

> formulated a Buddhist "catechism" in terms to which he felt (wrongly) all Buddhists could assent, persuaded the government to declare Vesak a public holiday, and encouraged Buddhists to celebrate it with songs modelled on Christmas carols—whence further developed the custom of sending Vesak cards on the analogy of Christmas cards. (Gombrich and Obeyesekere 1988:205)

Vesak is celebrated as the Buddha's Birthday, a further analogy with Christmas.

Since 1980, Vesak has been celebrated in Toronto as an all Buddhist ecumenical service under the sponsorship of the Buddhist Council of Canada. The different Buddhist groups must first agree on a suitable weekend date in May to celebrate the event, since the Theravada and Mahayana traditions celebrate Vesak on different days. The Vesak services celebrated in 1985 and 1986 followed roughly the same format and were both held in the Medical Sciences auditorium of the University of Toronto. Both services began with the chanting of the homage to the Buddha, the three refuges and the five precepts, all in Pali and conforming to the order of service followed by Theravada Buddhists. In 1986, the four vows were added in English. These vows are usually chanted in English as part of western Zen Buddhist services. In addition, two sutras printed in the program in English—the Great Discourse on Good Fortune and the Heart of Perfect Wisdom—were chanted in English. These sutras are also part of western Zen Buddhist services.

In 1985, the service was followed by a cultural program featuring dances, songs and art from various ethnic Buddhist associations. For example, the Lao community presented a Lao children's dance in the afternoon program. In 1986, this cultural program was not included, and instead a number of guest speakers addressed the much smaller audience in English and their own languages.

One event in most of the combined Buddhist services celebrating Vesak is the *kambutsu* ceremony, described as the bathing of a statue of the baby Buddha with holy water. The bathing of Buddhist images is an integral part of some Lao Buddhist services such as the New Year celebration but is not a standard part of all services. However, the act of bathing an image of a baby Buddha is a regular part of services in Chinese, Japanese and Korean Mahayana traditions. It is thus a ritual act that has related but not identical symbolic significance in both Theravada and Mahayana traditions. It is interesting to note that in 1985, this act was identified in the program as an ancient Chinese and Japanese ceremony, and in 1986, as an ancient Asian ceremony, reflecting, perhaps, an increased understanding of the base of shared ritual knowledge between the two traditions.

Although Lao monks have participated in the combined service, and Lao children in the cultural program, many Lao Buddhists who were active in Wat Lao expressed no interest in this service. Only 57 percent of the Lao respondents indicated having attended a Vesak celebration in Canada. Unfortunately, the question did not differentiate between Vesak as celebrated at Wat Lao and Vesak as sponsored by the Buddhist Council of Canada. Those few respondents (five) who attended a non-Lao "North American Buddhist service" may well have been referring to the celebration of Vesak sponsored by the Buddhist Council.

### Toward a Non-Sectarian Buddhism

The conversion of westerners from the Judeo-Christian tradition has encouraged and accelerated the integration of Theravada and Mahayana doctrine and practice seen in services such as Vesak. In this search for a non-sectarian Buddhism, adherents combine precepts and *sutras* in new formats, stripped of their markers of ethnic identification. These settings are understandable to western Buddhist converts but alien to Lao or Tibetan Buddhists, for example, whose Buddhist practice is deeply embedded in the cultural trappings of language, social exchange and familiar objects (cf. McLellan 1987).

In Britain and Europe, Theravada Buddhism was known first through the scholarly tradition of translation and analysis of texts. The Pali Text Society, established in 1881, furthered the knowledge of Buddhism, but the scholars translating the texts did not necessarily practice Buddhism. However, there were a number of Europeans who became monks as well as scholars. An Englishman, C. Bennet, studied Buddhism in Burma, ordained there and led the first Buddhist mission to England in 1908 (Rajavaramuni 1984:123).

In North America, many westerners first came in contact with a form of Mahayana Buddhism through the Zen writings of D. T. Suzuki (1956); but Zen meditation is often removed from its Buddhist base. Since the 1960s, Tibetan Buddhism has gained in popularity through the teachings of Chogyam Trungpa Tulku and Tarthang Tulku. The popularity of lay Buddhism grew primarily through these Mahayana practices, with Theravada Buddhism less well known except in Buddhist scholarly circles. However, recently the practice of Burmese meditation and that of the Thai forest monastery tradition has begun to attract western followers in England, North America and Australia. Following a period of meditation training, the disciples of teachers such as Achan Mun and Achan Chah in Thailand are transferring the forest monk tradition to western countries. This export Buddhism fuels the growth of nonsectarian or international Buddhism:

> Thanks to increasing cultural exchanges among countries, the emergence of international Buddhist associations, and the increasing flow of translations from both Mahayana and Theravada sources . . . misunderstandings are diminishing. (Blofeld 1971:7)

There are also transformations within national Buddhist communities reflecting an interchange of ideas and interpretations between Theravada and Mahayana traditions. In Thailand, Buddhadasa and the Suan Moke movement integrates materials from Mahayana Buddhism in teaching and meditation practice. This prolific thinker and writer uses Zen concepts such as emptiness to reinterpret Thai Buddhism. In addition, he has translated Zen sutras such as The Platform

Sutra of the Sixth Patriarch and The Teachings of Huang Po
into Thai and English. Sulak Sivaraksa uses the Pali concept
of *kalyanamitta* ,or good friend, to express relations between
Thai Buddhism and other religions. He argues that we must
look beyond Buddhist texts and national heritage to "find good
friends beyond one's national boundary and one's religious
affiliation" (Sivaraksa 1986:9). Within countries where
Theravada Buddhism is the majority religion, Mahayana
minorities adapt easily to the dominant tradition:

> In Cambodia, Laos, Thailand, and Burma,
> Mahayana draws strength from an environment in
> which almost everybody is Buddhist, but many
> families of Chinese or Vietnamese descent
> gradually become absorbed by the Theravadin form
> of Buddhism prevailing around them:  there is no
> rivalry between the two schools, and except for
> people living in tightly knit immigrant
> communities, it is often more convenient to adopt
> the religious forms of the local people. (Blofeld
> 1971:3)

However, Theravadin groups may be less interested in
international nonsectarian Buddhism not only because in North
America their religion is an important part of their ethnic
identity, but also because they have a greater need to ensure
the validity of the Theravadin ordination and monastic practice
in a new context. These are harder to monitor in non-
Theravadin countries and communities. However, Dumoulin
writes, "The Theravada tendency to approach other Buddhists
primarily in terms of conversion has been in evidence even on
ecumenical occasions" (Dumoulin 1976:59).

There have been sporadic moves toward the
establishment of nonsectarian Buddhist communities, both
from western Buddhists and from Asian Buddhists. In
England, the Friends of the Western Buddhist Order was
founded by the Venerable Sangharakshita, an Englishman who
took first the Theravada lower and higher ordination and then
the Bodhisattva Precepts as a Mahayana ordination. His
community ordains both men and women and has an amended
code of conduct suitable to the west (Rajavaramuni
1985:143–144).

These new interpretations of doctrine and practice are likely to influence Buddhism in the original homelands of Theravada Buddhism. The directions of change include an increased respect for lay participation in administration and ritual practice, more social activism and new religious roles for women, all influenced to some extent by the blurring of the sectarian boundaries between Theravada and Mahayana Buddhism.

# Chapter Six

## Adapting Buddhism

### Becoming a Minority Religion
*Adapting to their new environment is a matter of physical survival to them. Since they are in the minority, they must safeguard that which means the most to them. (Simon-Barouh 1983:17)*

The Lao in Toronto, like the Cambodians in Rennes described in the above quote, must adapt to a new religious landscape. For the first time—as individuals and as groups—Lao Buddhists represent a minority religion within a Judeo-Christian majority. Buddhism was almost universal and a state religion in both Laos and Cambodia. There is no cumulated cultural experience guiding either group (or any Theravadin group, for that matter) as to how to organize religious belief and practice as a small minority within a dominant and very different religious tradition. Although Mahayana groups have existed as minority religions within Theravadin countries, Theravadins in Southeast Asia have always had the dominant tradition within their respective countries. For the most part, the Theravada traditions have been national religions. How does this affect religious adaptation of Lao Buddhists in their countries of resettlement?

First, they have never had to operate without a clearly defined religious hierarchy with clearly defined leadership. Decisions now have to be made on an ad hoc basis with lay associations taking major initiatives. Second, they have never had to operate with so few religious resources—monks, texts, temples, shrines, equipment, knowledge and famous pilgrimage sites. Even the poorest Lao village would have had access to a monk and space suitable for merit making and ordination. Further, the accumulated experience of elderly villagers who had participated in past ritual events would guarantee transmission of knowledge about Buddhist practice and provide a critical commentary on ritual events. This experience is lacking in resettlement countries where many young adults settle after having spent ten or more years in refugee camps. Finally, Wat Lao, or any temple established in a North American city can no longer be the "hub" of community life; the physical space of the temple no longer dominates the landscape nor serves the multiple functions performed by a Lao temple in Laos. In Laos, the temple and Buddhist activities were totally integrated into everyday life. In Canada, the temple loses its centrality—spatially, cognitively and socially—because of the dispersed population and the economic effort Lao refugees need to expend to survive and prosper in North America.

**Recreating Buddhist Institutions**

Establishing a Sangha for Lao Buddhism outside Laos requires extraordinary flexibility and patience on the part of monks and laity. The Vinaya-Pitaka, one of the three baskets of the Pali canon, regulates all aspects of monastic life in Southeast Asia through 227 rules governing monks' everyday activities such as eating, dressing and hygiene and their relationship with laity and other monks. Many adjustments must be made to longstanding monastic custom, even if the item under discussion is not addressed in the Vinaya rules of monastic conduct. These adjustments may become the focus for community negotiation, as lay groups vie with one another to present an image of strict discipline. Laity view themselves as the guardians of monastic virtue and discipline. But it is not the laity who suffer if a Lao monk wears no shoes or no sweater on a cold winter day in a northern city.

Clothing adjustments must be made so that monks accustomed to wearing three cotton cloths can survive North American winters. Sweaters need to be worn under robes, and socks, shoes and boots worn for outside wear. Woolen hats cover shaved heads. In the past, practical adjustments to food, clothing and housing were regularly made as Buddhism spread from India into cold areas such as Tibet. Flexibility was built into the Sangha rules, and the Sangha was expected to respect the customs and observe the laws of regions where monks wandered. These practical adjustments may obscure other attempts to blend in with North American dress codes, for example, a monk who wears a clerical collar and a brown overcoat over his saffron robe (McAteer 1988:10).

The morning alms round (*bindabat*) is usually omitted in North America, except for alms collection before religious services. Food for the noon meal is either prepared in the monks' apartment by members of the temple committee or brought in by pious laywomen who arrange in advance to supply food for a particular day. In the day-to-day running of temples in North America, monks may occasionally make their own meals or prepare coffee or tea for themselves and occasionally for guests. There are no temple boys and few novices to perform these small tasks for monks. It is likely that the laity are more concerned about these breaches of normal etiquette than are the monks themselves. When questioning a monk who served me a cup of tea, he responded that his intention was to extend kindness to a visitor. He was, however, very careful not to hand the cup to me directly but to maintain all formality concerning interaction with a woman.

The centrality of food in Lao ceremonies cannot be overemphasized. Yet the relations between food and religious practice have been transformed in North America. On ritual occasions, there is an excess of food donated to the monks in the form of cooked glutinous rice, unpeeled fruit and special dishes such as curries and soups to be served with the rice. The rice and fruit are placed directly into the alms bowls of the monks. The other dishes are arranged on trays and presented to the monks. In fact, the monks take only a small amount from the dishes displayed on the trays, although they symbolically accept all the trays presented. This excess of food is redistributed to the laity in the form of a communal meal following the service. This is an important social and political occasion in North America, as it is one of the few occasions when Lao from distant suburbs and different communities get together. It may also be the only time some individuals and families consume traditional Lao food. The preparation of many of the dishes is very time consuming. For working women, these dishes may be too complicated and expensive to prepare on a regular basis. Herbs that would grow wild or be cultivated near Lao households are flown from Thailand in special shipments to a few grocery stores in Chinatown at exorbitant prices, comparatively speaking. However, many Lao households still grow their own herbs and share them with (or sell them to) their friends.

Other lay concerns surround the monks' use of objects such as cars and telephones that were never covered by the original Vinaya rules. Their use is not regulated, but some individuals feel that monks should not be taking driving lessons or conducting business on the telephone. These are, however, necessary adjustments to North American life-styles.

## Ritual Transformations

For Lao Buddhism to flourish in North America, a great number of changes have to occur in Buddhist practice. Most striking to an outside observer is the tolerance and flexibility shown by the monks and by the lay Buddhist committees working with the temples in North America. Many of the inevitable disagreements and tensions have not emerged publicly in my presence, although they undoubtedly exist in every community. Although more traditional elderly Lao who remember vividly the way rituals used to be carried out may point out differences between the way things are done in Canada and in Laos, they tolerate the compromises that have been made and appear active in the construction of new ritual traditions more suited for North American community life.

In Theravadin communities in Southeast Asia, there is no formal joining of a congregation, no public conversion to Buddhism. As suggested earlier, formal conversion or reconversion may be one innovation Buddhist communities adopt in North America. One Vietnamese refugee, raised in a Buddhist home in Vietnam, said that he did not formally embrace Buddhism until five years after he arrived in Canada (McAteer 1988:10).

In the course of a Lao Buddhist ritual, the adaptations to North American contexts are subtle and suitable: marigolds substitute for gold-colored flowers available in Laos; religious items brought from Thailand are smaller in size and not in local Lao style; incense and candles are more carefully protected, since the danger of fire on the top floor of a crowded apartment building has different consequences than fire on an open porch in Laos. Residents also fear that smoke could set off smoke detector alarms and alert neighbors to the fact that unfamiliar religious rituals are taking place next door.

During rituals, reference is made to North American locations as well as Lao locations. A meditation exercise, for example, spread loving-kindness through the body of the mediator, the room where meditation took place, the suburb, city, province, country and finally, the rest of the world. When visitors attended services, they were included as "friends in the *dhamma*." However, in Lao services very little English was ever used except occasionally for a phrase referring to a government regulation.

The mechanics of carrying out *kruat nam*, or water blessing, are altered when the ritual act takes place indoors. In Laos, holy water is often poured directly onto the ground or onto growing plants, with no water saved for other purposes. In North America, water is brought into the hall in bottles, poured into silver bowls and poured back into bottles. Many families take large containers of water blessed by the monks—even gallon jugs—home with them. This water maybe shared among family members and friends unable to come to the service and may also be kept for several months until another monk is in the community.

Other adjustments are made to conform to host-country regulations. In Laos, monks do not perform wedding ceremonies, although they may be invited to merit-making celebrations before or after the lay service. Lao couples in Canada could simply register their marriage in a civil ceremony and be married according to Lao custom. But marriage is of great concern to civil authorities, and in some countries, such as Australia, Buddhism is not recognized as a religion. Although Mahayana monks officiate at marriage ceremonies, these are not considered legal marriages. Officials may well assume that Mahayana and Theravada monks "do" the same things and may seek to regulate their involvement in civil rituals. Marriages are simply not of concern to Buddhist monks.

Funerals, however, are the direct concern of monks and are the focus of much Buddhist ritual. Memorial services one hundred days and one year after the death are also occasions of Buddhist merit-making activity. In North America, the Lao may also be cremated, as was their custom in Laos. However, in many communities the Lao must also use a funeral home to meet government regulations. Often, visitation time is too short for the Lao, who would prefer to stay with the body and the family all night, if possible. In Rockford, Illinois, the resident monks conduct a Buddhist funeral service at the funeral home and also at the family home of the deceased. There, both Christian priest and Buddhist priest may perform funeral services together (Engebretson 1983). Even without a monk, Theravada Buddhists have been accommodated in North American funeral parlors. A Cambodian woman needed to perform a small ritual to cleanse the mouth of her deceased husband. In the words of an observer:

The undertaker stood next to me to witness and share in this beautiful ceremony. The foster son began to chant. The mother poured the special water into her husband's mouth and continued to chant with her son. We were only there a few minutes. It was very simple, it wasn't anything complex, and it didn't take a lot of time. But you could just see the relief in this woman. She really needed to do this to be able to deal with the loss of her husband. You could just see the peace that came over her as she performed this ritual for her husband. (Battisti 1989:89)

Time is an essential attribute of ritual. Buddhist ritual transferred to North America undergoes several temporal transformations. In general, time in Lao communities is conceptually similar to perceptions of time elsewhere in Southeast Asia (cf. Geertz 1967). Time in these village communities is perceived more as a quality—auspicious or inauspicious—than a quantity to be measured. Time is a quality determined by the intersection of repeating cycles—lunar, agricultural and ritual—with human events such as weddings or funerals. Rituals in Buddhist Southeast Asia reflect two kinds of temporal cycles: the first, the sacred biography of the Buddha; the second, the agricultural cycle of planting and harvesting rice. These cycles have stabilized enough to encourage the institutionalization of the seasonal round of events in the Buddhist ritual calendar. However, even in Theravada Buddhist countries, the ritual cycle can be altered, depending on external events or internal politics. Some rituals are stressed, others unstressed. For example, new cropping patterns may alter and usually reduce the time available for communal ritual events. In Thailand, events like Kathin and Raek Naa Khwan (first ploughing ceremony) appear to have increased in importance or been revived after a period of decline. While the Lao ritual cycle in North America reflects the ritual cycle in Laos, some rituals are emphasized more than others. Other changes are related to the concept of time imposed by North American living.

Institutional time, shaped by dependence on bureaucracies and schedules, has influenced the Lao use of weekends for ritual observances. Shifting from the lunar cycle determining *wan sin* and seasonal celebrations to the weekly cycle, the Lao must now integrate their ritual observances with their workweeks. Services are generally held on Sundays in Toronto and other cities where Buddhist and Christian services are in opposition or there is competition within the community making it difficult to participate in both ritual systems on a single weekend. However, in Rockford, Illinois, Buddhist services are often held on Saturday, freeing refugees to attend Christian services, often with their sponsors, on Sundays. However, if the Lao choose to join a Christian church, they are expected to break with Buddhist practice (Engebretson 1983:83).

When the weekend becomes the focus for ritual activity, then it becomes more difficult to schedule ritual events on weekends that do not conflict with the ritual events of other Buddhist groups. Ordinations and other personal rites of passage must be scheduled to fit into weekends, school vacations or leaves of absence from work. Auspicious times and dates become less significant as institutional time takes precedence over ritual time. The need for schedules and firm reservations requires planning ahead for hall rentals, for example. And although events may not take place "on time" according to western perceptions of time, events are more constrained temporally as halls need to be cleaned up and emptied out quickly when they are rented by the hour.

In North America, ritual events are condensed in time. Rituals that lasted three days in Laos take one day in North America. All-day rituals in Laos are condensed to two or three hours in North America. This is partly related to the shift to the weekend, when there are alternative ways to spend time. Rituals compete with sports and other leisure activities carried out on weekends; in Laos, ritual time replaced work time. In North America, other social, economic and political activities of the Lao are embedded within ritual time. Since there are only a limited number of occasions for the widely dispersed Lao groups in southern Ontario to get together, Buddhist rituals are also occasions for visiting, matchmaking, selling cloth from Laos and exchanging information about available jobs and apartments. Like other westerners, the Lao are soon forced to have their temporal structures tightly embedded, as more activities have to be crammed into one day. This "busyness" alters the quality of ritual time. The longer time spent in ritual action enhances the reality and meaning of the event for the participants. In lengthy rituals spread over several days, the pace of ritual is coterminous with the pace of everyday life, as if the broader cycles of cosmic time are in conjunction with ordinary everyday time, as if the gods and spirits are among the participants (J. Van Esterik 1978:4). In these extended rituals, it is perfectly acceptable to move in and out of concentrated attention, to leave and chat; however, the more condensed versions assume everyone must concentrate attentively because the ritual will be "finished" in one hour.

A final temporal change concerns the opportunistic nature of scheduling and embedding ritual events. When monks are only available occasionally, ritual cycles change to accommodate their schedules. Seasonal rituals may be stressed or unstressed depending on the availability of monks. On the occasion of a single monk's visit to a community, a public ritual might be held on Sunday, a house blessing at a sponsor's home the next day and a service to dispel bad luck at a third house. This opportunistic scheduling means that ritual acts that may normally never occur together in Laos will be put together in North America. The seasonal cycle described in Chapter Four reflects some of these embedded ritual activities.

These examples of scheduling, condensation and embeddedness in ritual time may be quite disorienting for elderly Lao familiar with the more leisurely pace of ritual time in Laos. However, since most Lao in North America experienced the disruptions of normal time during the war and the suspension of time while in refugee camps, they may adapt readily to the temporal structures of future-oriented westerners, even within their religious domain.

## Transmission of Buddhist Knowledge

When there are no monks available in a community to provide consultation and ritual services, there is no reason to assume that the Lao are no longer practicing Buddhists. For example, 81.6 percent of respondents said that they prayed at home, 34.6 percent meditated and 38.5 percent kept eight precepts on certain days. Of course, these responses are from a sample of Lao who are already committed to Buddhist practice, since they were attending a service when the survey was distributed. These are successful short-term strategies for maintaining Buddhism as a system of ethics and morality. However, these strategies do not address the long-term need to teach Buddhism as a total religious system to the younger generation.

The transmission of Buddhist knowledge is particularly problematic for Theravadin refugee communities. Members of the Lao Buddhist Association are anxious for young people to be taught the fundamentals of Lao Buddhism, ideally by a monk. A major concern among Quebec Lao is that their children be taught Buddhism (Dorais and Pilon-Lê 1988:226). Some of these concerns are reflected in the modifications made to the ritual procedures described above. For example, monks can no longer assume that most of the laity know the chants and responses making up Buddhist services. Currently, there are several men who were formerly monks who know chants and ritual procedures very well. In Lao services, monks occasionally explain the history and meaning of certain activities and events such as Pradabdin, as if realizing that many Lao attending the service may have forgotten or may be unfamiliar with the ritual as it was practiced in Laos. In Buddhist services where English and Pali are used, monks often explain the chants in English before they are recited and break the Pali responses into shorter phrases to ease memorizing the phrases. These adjustments are common in ecumenical Buddhist services and will be increasingly necessary as younger people who have had little formal Buddhist training form the majority of future congregations.

The dilemma faced by Lao Buddhists in North America concerning the transmission of Buddhist knowledge to children is shared by other Buddhist groups. The development of Buddhist Sunday schools for children did not develop spontaneously in Buddhist countries. When children were constantly exposed to rituals in the home and community and taught from sermons and moral teaching in the schools, there was no need for such institutions. The idea of Buddhist Sunday schools emerged from the Buddhist Theosophical Society organized by Europeans and Americans in the late 1800s. The society founded and ran Buddhist Sunday schools in Sri Lanka, supplying villages with textbooks, examinations, certificates and prizes emulating Christian Sunday schools (Gombrich and Obeyesekere 1988:205). Perhaps this model of Sunday schools will also be adopted in North America. The

Sri Lankan Buddhist community in Toronto already has a well-established program of teaching children. However, it is clear that this is not the way adult immigrants and refugees from Buddhist countries learned about their religious traditions. In a survey question asking where respondents learned most of their knowledge about Buddhism, 41 percent of all respondents identified parents, 35 percent identified monks and 24 percent mentioned school as sources of knowledge about Buddhism.

Other means of transmitting Buddhist knowledge have been developed in North America. Almost all services are videotaped. These tapes are made by the sponsor of the ritual or a local association and can be borrowed from the sponsor or the temple. They are shared with friends who could not attend the ritual. Sermons or *dhamma* lessons from visiting monks are taped and played on local radio stations. Dorais (1989) describes a Vietnamese spirit cult ritual that took place in Montreal where a cassette tape of a hymn recorded during ceremonies in southern California provided the music. The music should be played by two musicians and a singer, but no one in Montreal was able to perform. Video and cassette tapes may assist in preserving and transmitting ritual knowledge for the transitional generation growing up in refugee camps. However, Buddhist groups will have to develop new means of transmitting Buddhist teachings in the future.

This chapter has briefly reviewed some problems faced by Lao Buddhists in adapting their religious traditions to North America: consecrating temples that can be used for ordinations; establishing a legitimate ordination tradition with an unambiguous lineage; adjusting monastic rules to new social, economic, political and physical contexts; creating synchrony between ritual time and work schedules; transmitting Buddhist knowledge; and negotiating tensions resulting from monastic and lay differences in emphasis on *dana* (giving), *sila* (morality) and *bhavana* (wisdom). These problems are not unique to Buddhism in North America. The adaptations discussed here are themselves rooted in longstanding systems of discourse and debate within Theravada Buddhism. The debates replay themselves in discussions of Burmese Buddhism (Spiro 1970), Sri Lankan Buddhism (Gombrich and Obeyesekere 1988) and Thai Buddhism (Tambiah 1970, 1984). Theravada Buddhism encourages a multiplicity of modes of lay and monastic practice—merit making, meditation, devotion, keeping moral precepts—and even tolerates magical practices. The problems Lao Buddhists face in North America are at the core of Theravada Buddhism as it is practiced throughout the world. What is unique to the Lao case is not the foreign environment in which Buddhism is practiced but the suffering caused by the refugee experience itself, a topic developed in the following chapter.

# Chapter Seven

## Buddhism and Mental Health

### The Reduction of Suffering

*When, however, a society officially subscribes, as Canada does, to an ideology of multiculturalism, and the concept of adaptation is defined accordingly, the expectations in regard to the cultural adaptation of refugees and immigrants are far less stringent. Immigrants are at least encouraged to maintain some elements of their cultural traditions and no objections, official or otherwise, are raised when they settle in the same neighborhood. (Neuwirth and Rogge 1988:279)*

Canada's multicultural policy expressed in the Multiculturalism Act of 1988 aims to preserve the heritage of groups that enter Canada. It is no surprise to find that rhetoric does not always match reality. However, multicultural rhetoric breaks down most quickly in the area of religion. While church-state distinctions may be necessary and even clear-cut in some cases, the distinctions are particularly problematic where therapeutic strategies for maintaining health are expressed within a Buddhist idiom. The mental health of refugees from Southeast Asia is a good case in point. But we may not need to look to Buddhist ideology to understand these linkages between health and religion. Within the Judeo-Christian tradition, the words *healthy* and *holy* have a common linguistic root, and *religion* comes from the Latin verb *religio—*to bind back together. One of the most important therapeutic practices among the Lao is the act of binding performed during the *soukhouan* ritual, discussed again in this chapter to reinforce the importance of indigenous ritual as a mental health resource for Southeast Asian refugees in North America.

While religion and ritual are rarely considered in research on refugee resettlement, mental health problems and possible solutions are prominent in the analysis of the refugee experience. Bibliographies on refugee issues usually include a substantial section on mental health problems and services (cf. Ashmun 1983, 54 references). *Refugee Abstracts* includes substantial references under the categories of mental health and psychological problems. Beiser (1988b), in his review of the literature on migrant mental health, lists 271 references on the topics of measures of mental health status, factors affecting mental health status, migrants at risk and mental health services for immigrants and refugees. There is very little doubt that the stress of refugee migration has been recognized as a contributing factor in a wide range of psychopathologies including depression, psychoses and neurotic disorders (cf. Beiser 1988a,b; Berry 1987;Engelsmann 1988).

In the camps of first asylum, mental health problems of refugees are not easily addressed. Camps must deal first with immediate problems of security, shelter, food and medical emergencies, leaving little opportunity for the development of counseling programs or preventive mental health measures. Since camps are intended to be emergency, short-term solutions for refugees, there are seldom adequate facilities for dealing with mental health problems or preventive programmes. As Chan (1990) points out, camps are more often geared to custodial goals than to the psychosocial needs of refugees. In the Thai camps, service providers speak with fear about the possibilities of mass suicide, while they try to deal with the reality of single suicides of individuals rejected for resettlement or unable to cope with their suffering. Each suicide provides opportunities for others to compare their situation with that of the suicide victim and to consider trying the same alternative. In the context of well-developed beliefs about spirits and ghosts among Southeast Asians, rumors of people being possessed by the spirit of the deceased who then encourages others to kill themselves emphasize the fragile mental balance of many refugees in camp conditions.

The high social and psychological costs of long-term confinement in closed camps are almost inevitable considering the nature of the refugee experience. The combination of deprivation of food, funds and freedom along with unpredictable violence, as well as the fear of further violence—particularly for women—are serious risk factors for Southeast Asian refugees in Thai camps. Camp life for the Lao was characterized by boredom, depression, frustration and helplessness. Yet, when mental health staff and services were available in camps, refugee patients showed only "psychosocial adjustment reactions," rather than major psychiatric disorders as seen in refugee patients where there were no or few resident mental health staff available (Jilek 1988:4). This suggests that there may be effective patterns of coping strategies even in the worst of camp conditions.

The conditions of life in refugee camps have been illustrated in media presentations. Perhaps the most serious conditions exist among the Khmer refugees in the United Nations Border Relief Operation (UNBRO) border camps in Thailand. Here the risk factors were increased because of the trauma of starvation, torture and death of relatives under the Khmer Rouge regime. Although the Lao did not face the same severity of trauma, the observations made by mental health workers in the UNBRO border camps have some relevance to Lao camps as well. Mollica identifies cultural, spiritual and moral deprivation as risk factors contributing to the development of serious psychiatric illness among refugees in the Khmer border camps. He sees this deprivation as preventing the development of adequate coping behavior, especially for children and teenagers (Mollica 1990:135). Mollica's recommendations for community interventions acknowledge the importance of religion in establishing and maintaining adequate mental health. His recommendations include strictly enforcing the UN prohibitions against religious proselytizing in the camps and expanding the role of Buddhist monks, nuns and temples in the provision of mental health services. He argues that an improved new system of psychiatric care " should emphasize a partnership between traditional healing methods, Buddhism, and western approaches toward diagnosis and treatment" (Mollica 1990:145). He recognizes the need to strengthen the ability of UNBRO's monks to teach traditional healing and meditation practices and suggests that

> UNBRO should formally request the Buddhist temples and UNBRO monks to develop new healing rituals and rites for cleansing sexually abused women, including teenagers and children. Although such a ceremony does not exist in the Buddhist canon, senior Khmer monks abroad argue that the latter may be possible.

He also suggests the possibility of using Buddhist nuns and the convent to support and counsel rape victims (Mollica 1990:149).

While the suggestion regarding Buddhist healing rituals may not have been raised with a full understanding of Khmer concepts of sexuality and Buddhist practice, the recommendations acknowledge the importance of Buddhism for the mental health of refugees.

In spite of the substantial research done on acculturative stress of immigrants and refugees, the results are somewhat paradoxical:

> Roughly half of all scientifically credible studies suggest that immigrants and refugees do have higher rates of disorder than the host populations: the other half indicate that the rates are either equal or, in a few cases, that migrants actually have less disorder than indigenes. . . . The data suggests that trying to find one's way in a new country is a condition which puts mental health at risk. But, risk is not destiny. The contingencies which surround the experience determine whether one becomes a mental health statistic or a healthy, contributing member of society. (Beiser 1988a: 200)

Beiser refers to the ethnocultural community as one of the most powerful of those contingencies and identifies sociocultural support as one of the most effective measures for preventing mental ill health. But for Lao refugees in North American cities, the "ethnocultural community" may be difficult to access. With Lao refugees isolated in public housing apartment complexes in different parts of the city, with competing associations representing different regional and political allegiances, the Lao Buddhist Association and Wat Lao may provide the most viable sociocultural support beyond the network of immediate kin.

Westermeyer and Wintrob suggest how Buddhist ceremonies may offer support to Lao refugees:

> From a sociocultural perspective the threat of mental illness . . . can be seen as reinforcing attitudes and behaviors that are highly valued by Lao people. These include respect for ancestors and the environment, harmonious relations with family and friends, and the need for episodic respites from worry and work. (Westermeyer and Wintrob 1979:904)

Lao ceremonies provide opportunities to pay respect to the ancestors, strengthen relations with family and friends and relax and enjoy life. In the descriptions of ceremonies carried out in Toronto, certain core practices may be identified as being particularly effective in transmitting key Lao values as well as offering preventive strategies for mental health problems. These core practices include the *baci* or *soukhouan* ritual, *kruat nam* and feeding monks. Although *soukhouan* has been secularized and politicized in the present Lao regime, the latter two practices, more embedded in Buddhist practice, were ridiculed by the current LPDR regime: "The absurdity of pouring water to transfer merit was emphasized, and the idea that merit could be gained by feeding lazy, unworthy monks was scornfully dismissed" (Stuart-Fox and Bucknell 1982:70). Yet all three practices contain symbolic messages that have been condensed through performative action to summarize key Lao values.

I suggest that these values remain strong in the resettled Lao communities in North America among practicing Buddhists, converted Christians and acculturated Lao who profess no religious affiliation. Buddhist lowland Lao have performed these ritual acts for centuries; the values that underlie these actions continue to guide everyday life and to transmit the core of Lao identity to Lao refugees resettled in North America. Dorais and Pilon-Lê (1988) stress how core Lao rituals reinforce social and familial solidarity and provide the North American equivalent of village solidarity. At one level, these practices may be interpreted as components of rituals—components that may be added to or deleted from the structural "grammar" of Lao ceremonies. At another level, they may be understood as metaphors or models of Lao cultural identity that have been used by the Lao throughout the stages of the refugee experience—escape, camp life and resettlement. Ritual acts as metaphor "carry over" a particular framework or perspective from one domain of experience to another. These ritual metaphors reflect the dominant ethical preoccupations of the Lao and the problems they face in adapting to a new society. These problems include forming and maintaining groups, sharing resources, demonstrating moral worth and consolidating Lao identity.

*Soukhouan reasserts and strengthens social bonds by helping individuals "pull themselves together," and by tying individuals to their communities.*

*Soukhouan*, described in Chapter Four, is a part of almost all household, community and official ceremonies among the Lao. During the course of the ritual, the thirty-two components that make up a human are invited and enticed to return and reside comfortably and permanently in an individual. At the individual level, the strings tied by the elders around the wrist of the person for whom the ceremony is performed re-establish the psychological equilibrium of the individual, bring blessings and promote good health (Ngaosyvathn 1990:289).

As the strings help individuals "pull themselves together" in the face of challenges, so too the strings tie individuals more tightly into the community. The ceremony also re-establishes the equilibrium of the community and can only be accomplished in the presence of others. Ngaoysvathn outlines how *soukhouan* entails respect and social acceptance for the person undergoing the ritual, affirms the solidarity of those participating in it and may act to reintegrate individuals into their families and communities (Ngaoysvathn 1990:289–90). Through participating in *soukhouan*, Lao are made aware in a positive way of the ties binding them to their families and friends.

*Soukhouan*, as a joint social activity, affirms core Lao values of reciprocity and sociability. Ngaosvathn writes that *soukhouan*

> expresses traditional Lao values of avoidance of conflict and aims at promoting consensus within the social fabric and strengthening social ties. As a key element of Lao culture, the ritual is a microcosm of Lao values serving to integrate the individual both spiritually and socially. In these terms, the ritual may be seen as the quintessential expression of conceptualizations of Lao identity. (Ngaoysvathn 1990:300)

*Soukhouan* rituals present great analytical problems or challenges for anthropologists because they require examination once again of the relations between different aspects of religious and cultural practice; *soukhouan* encompasses animistic, Buddhist and Brahmanic concepts in a single ritual event. The ritual is widespread among Tai peoples.

The problem of where spirits and Hindu deities fit into Theravada Buddhist practice is epitomized in *soukhouan* rituals. To some extent, the potential contradictions are also resolved, for in the practice of *soukhouan*, the strands are truly interwoven and bound together in the performative act. The questions raised by analysts regarding whether *soukhouan* is a Buddhist, animist or Brahmanic ritual are not raised by participants, nor are the questions relevant to them.

Anthropologists persist in separating the historical, textual and contextual strands of Theravada Buddhism, spirit worship and court Brahmanism. In different contexts, one strand predominates or provides the dominant symbol for religious activities. Currently the symbols of court Brahmanism are effectively purged from the Lao religious scene. Kingship no longer exists as the pivotal reference point for ritual behavior as it still is in Thailand. Nevertheless, the more formal *baci* invokes the Hindu gods to observe and participate in the *soukhouan*.

The act of performing a *soukhouan* integrates and demonstrates the interdependence of all the strands of Lao religion. Some Lao have the knowledge and power to separate out certain symbols to make political statements. The Pathet Lao, after their unsuccessful efforts to destroy religion altogether, are now skilled in pulling apart the strands to emphasize one and downplay another. Since there is no Lao king, there is no need for "royal style" rituals (cf. P. Van Esterik 1980b), and hence royal symbols have probably disappeared or been reinterpreted in Laos. The decision to reduce the lavishness of these rituals by fiat was superfluous, since there was no need for royal style rituals any more. Symbols of royalty held no meaning in the new social and political order.

The greatest contradiction between the various strands in Lao religion concerns the person. Theravada Buddhism is based on concepts of *anatta* (nonself) and *anicca* (impermanence). How can these concepts provide the basis for stable social and political systems with people arranged in stable hierarchies (or unstable ones in recent years) and institutions of some permanence? *Soukhouan* fixes the temporary manifestation we perceive as humans long enough to "tie

down" this human illusion with all its suffering and imperfec-
tions and gives it a fixed, bounded identity. Building on the
insightful work of Condominas (1987), we can use the
concept of embôitment to stress the importance of the body or
person as the first "box," surrounded sequentially by the
household, village and *muang* (political realm, princedom or
city). It is the body that is most immediately addressed in
*soukhouan* rituals.

The *soukhouan*, the most basic Lao ritual, stresses the
integrity and identity of persons and offers ritual protection to
keep these mobile "souls" trapped within a person's body.
Only then can a person act (morally or immorally) within a
Buddhist social order. Lao are not ambiguous about nonself
and impermanence as guiding principles. They place priority
on the integrity of the person as a social actor. Thus, they have
been able to carry the ritual guaranteeing this integrity across
revolutions and resettlement virtually unchanged.

The loss of "soul," vital essence or *khouan* is a powerful
metaphor for the refugee experience, as individuals are
separated from their homeland and loved ones and are facing
painful disruptions to every aspect of their lives. Like the
wandering souls unable to return to their homes, refugees
wander without homes, facing dangerous and unknown
conditions. *Soukhouan* rituals are particularly necessary when
the social order has been disrupted, as in the experience of
refugee flight and resettlement. As in the Lao refugee
communities throughout North America, it is the strength of
these social bonds that can tie souls into bodies and reintegrate
individuals into new community settings—in refugee camps,
North American cities and, for repatriated Lao, the
transformed villages of the Lao People's Democratic
Republic.

***Kruat Nam*** *extends compassion and loving-kindness and*
*transfers merit to all sentient beings.*

At every *wan sin* service and services to commemorate
the dead (including funerals), the merit accrued by meritorious
acts, most commonly feeding monks, is shared with others.
Merit transference is stressed whenever there is a rupture in
the social order such as during funerals and ordinations; for
refugees, the rupture in the social order is particularly
obvious. Transferring merit is one of the ten traditional good

deeds of Theravada Buddhism (Gombrich and Obeyesekere 1988:24). The sharing of merit with the gods and with the wandering ghosts (Pali: *peta*), who are the only nonhumans who can acquire merit, is mentioned in Buddhist scriptures (Anguttara-Nikaya, *sutra* 50; Digha-Nikaya, *sutra* 16). But the transfer of merit can easily slip into a less sophisticated and more mechanical explanation to sidestep the fact that each individual must take full responsibility for his or her fate. In practice, the act is a very human response to the loss of loved ones and the uncertainty of their rebirth status. The practice, then, is well established in Theravada Buddhism. And even for those unfamiliar with the canonical arguments about "dependent origination," alternative rationales exist. Those include the Pali concept of *pattidana*, or rejoicing in giving. The people who perform meritorious acts generously wish that others—particularly their deceased relatives—could reap the benefits of their meritorious deeds. For the Thai and the Lao this wish is most intensively directed toward deceased parents.

This act of generosity is particularly poignant for refugees who may have been separated from their parents before they had opportunities to transfer merit to them. For others, close relatives remain missing and are presumed dead. Few refugees in North America can afford to return to Laos at short notice in time for their parents' funerals. With limited comparative data, I would suggest that the act of transferring merit is more significant for Lao refugees than for Lao Buddhists in Laos. During the service celebrating the beginning of Buddhist rains retreat in a temple in Vientiane, Laos, in July 1989, the act was performed very quickly with water poured onto plants and over cobblestones much more casually than in Toronto services. There was not the emotional intensity and tension during the chanting that one feels among Lao refugees in Toronto.

This practice also reflects core Lao values regarding responsibilities to elders and parents. These responsibilities do not end with resettlement in a third country. In fact, they become more complex, as the Lao in Canada must deal with parents left in Laos or in refugee camps in Thailand, missing parents, parents whose funerals and memorial services were incomplete and elderly relatives who require care in Canada. For example, an unmarried Lao refugee in Toronto who could not support his elderly parents placed his parents in a subsidized seniors' apartment where neither he nor their grandchildren could stay overnight for a visit. The old couple felt imprisoned—isolated and useless because they were cut off from their relatives. But regulations in the apartments made it impossible for the unmarried son to fulfill his responsibilities to his parents (Gordon 1990:90).

*Kruat nam* is a metaphor of loss and death. It expresses one of the dominant ethical preoccupations of Lao refugees and exemplifies the kind of problems they face in adapting to their new home. With the loss of their parental and ancestral generations, they lose the direct continuity with their past that is at the core of Lao identity. For Lao Buddhists in North America, the practice of transferring merit to deceased relatives helps bridge the distance between Laos and Canada, past and present, old and new responsibilities.

**Liang Phra** *celebrates reciprocity and the benefits of sharing with others.*

Following Buddhist services and for all household rituals where monks are present, food offered to the monks is redistributed to the laity in the form of a communal meal. This is more than just the near-universal commensality of most social occasions, for it is considered a particular blessing to share the food given to and accepted by the monks. Anyone participating in the ritual occasion is welcome and encouraged to join the groups of friends sitting around raised bamboo trays laden with special Lao food dishes. Food is politely served to neighbors first and eaten in a slightly more reflective and less rambunctious manner than what might be seen at an ordinary Lao party. Even those who have not contributed food—particularly those who have not contributed food—are actively encouraged to share the meal, as if the sharing of food may cause the intention to give generously to arise among all partaking of the meal. Leftover food is carefully wrapped and taken to those who were unable to attend the ceremony, so that they too may participate in the blessings created by the communal merit making.

It is difficult to be a Lao in North America and difficult to form a Lao community. People who arrive in North American cities together may not have known each other in the camps in Thailand, let alone in Laos. They share a national origin and the refugee experience and little else. From this commonality, they must construct Lao identity and Lao community.

Lao associations help with the task of making connections between people, often based on their home region in Laos. Social occasions provide opportunities to search for connections—prominent families known in common, friends of friends. But Buddhist ritual occasions provide special opportunities for forming and strengthening groups. The problem of dealing with strangers is a problem of trust. Who is trustworthy? Who shares your personal standards of morality? Who is a true friend? Buddhist merit making is an opportunity for displaying one's moral worth and demonstrating one's trustworthiness. In refugee camps and in countries of asylum, the need to know who to trust is even greater than in rural Lao villages. Survival strategies are based on being able to rely on other Lao for moral and material support. Central to Lao identity is that Lao help each other. Values of reciprocity and sharing are extremely important to the Lao. In the strongly individualized and materialistic communities of North America, it is particularly difficult to maintain models of generosity and reciprocity. Commensality—the shared meal of Buddhist merit makers—is a model of reciprocity, redistribution and generosity and actually creates groups. The act of eating together and sharing each other's food constitutes groups even if the group identity can only be maintained for a short period of time and must be reconstituted on the next ritual occasion. However, it is a concrete and reliable means of establishing a moral community where people know they can develop relations of trust with others and cooperate in joint activities within the domain of religion and in other domains.

## Conclusions

Lao rituals recreate moments from a mythical past to legitimate the uncertain present. The three ritual acts described in this last chapter had meaning when they were embedded in the royal state rituals of the Kingdom of Laos. They lost much of that meaning when royal centers disappeared or lost their sanctity. But they accumulated other meanings as they were transformed in the secular non-Buddhist socialist state of the LPDR. And they have acquired yet newer meanings in North American contexts. The Lao, in addition to the crisis of "loss and load" shared by all refugees, face particularly difficult problems resolving the meaning of what it means to be Lao outside of Laos. These ritual acts are the raw materials from which individual Lao refugees can begin to structure a new Lao identity in North America. From these ritual acts they select those values that are central to their individual and collective identities as Lao refugees (not Southeast Asian or Indochinese refugees).

Buddhism is important to this task because it provides a framework for explaining suffering and for making sense out of an otherwise chaotic world. Buddhism, by transforming fatality into continuity (Anderson 1983:18), links the living, the dead and the unborn in Laos and in the new homelands of resettled Lao. The suffering of the refugees "is not limited to the pain of losing family and country: it is deepened by awareness that former cultural solutions, the blueprints for action and interpretation of the world that one learned from childhood, cannot be trusted" (Muecke 1987:275).

When the Lao became refugees, they left the land where they were born and raised. That land sustained them physically, providing them with food and shelter. This loss of land as a subsistence base we acknowledge in the provision of emergency resources such as shelter and food to meet the refugees' immediate needs. But what of the other capacities of the land? The land also contained guardian spirits of localities, ancestors' ashes, relics and sacred places of pilgrimage. Bakhtin (1981) refers to these as chronotypes—points in the geography of a community where time and space intersect and fuse. The spiritual resources of sacred geography are unseen; their loss unacknowledged. But the land has a distinct meaning when the territory affects people's bodily substances, their spiritual essences (cf. Daniel 1984:9). And these resources of locality are never replaced, cannot ever be replaced except refugees who are repatriated. Spiritual losses go unrecognized in the face of more visible material losses.

Buddhist rituals conducted in new lands cannot reconstitute the religious institutions of Laos, nor do they yet represent a North American hybrid form of religious practice. Identities in limbo, Lao Buddhists refer back not to the Laos they fled from but back to an "imagined community" (cf. Anderson 1983), the Laos that never was: the Laos that was never a colony of France; the Laos that was never saturation-bombed in the 1960s and 1970s; the Laos that is not struggling with the task of repairing a war torn-economy and transforming itself into a self-sufficient socialist state. The model for this ritual identity is embedded in myth. This book opened with a brief account of the history of Laos, beginning with the story of Prince Fa Ngum, the founder of the Kingdom of Lan Xang. Ritual time allows for the restoration of the Kingdom of Lan Xang at the height of its power under Prince Fa Ngum, if even for a few hours, in the basements of subsidized housing projects and community centers across North America.

# References Cited

Adelman, H., ed. (1982). Canada and the Indochinese Refugees. Regina: L. A. Wiegl Educational Associates.

Anderson, B. (1983). Imagined Communities. London: Verso Editions.

Archaimbault, C. (1971). The New Year Ceremony at Basak (South Laos). S. Boas, trans. Ithaca, N.Y.: Cornell University Southeast Asia Program.

Ashmun, L. (1983). Resettlement of Indochinese Refugees in the United States: A Selective Bibliography. Monograph Series on Southeast Asia, Center for Southeast Asian Studies, Northern Illinois University, DeKalb, Illinois.

Ba, T. Q. (1988). The Indochinese of Southeast New Brunswick. In Ten Years Later: Indochinese Communities in Canada. L.-J. Dorais, K. B. Chan and D. M. Indra, eds. Montreal: Canadian Asian Studies Association.

Bakhtin, M. (1981). The Dialogic Imagination: Four Essays. M. Holquist, ed. Austin: University of Texas Press.

Battisti, R. (1989). Preserving the Spiritual and Cultural Heritage of Amerasian and Southeast Asian Families. In Reasons for Living and Hoping: The Spiritual and Psycho-Social Needs of Southeast Asian Refugee Children and Youth Resettled in the United States. Washington, D.C.: The International Catholic Child Bureau, Inc.

Beiser, M. (1988a). The Mental Health of Immigrants and Refugees in Canada. Santé Culture Health, vol. 5, pp. 197–213.

135

Beiser, M. ed. (1988b). After the Door Has Been Opened:
Mental Health Issues Affecting Immigrants and
Refugees in Canada. Report of the Canadian Task
Force on Mental Health Issues Affecting Immigrants
and Refugees. Copublished by Health and Welfare
Ottawa, Canada.

Benyasut, M. (1989). The Ecology of Phanat Nikhom Camp.
Bangkok: Institute of Asian Studies, Chulalongkorn
University.

Bernstein, S. (1989). Reflections on What It Means to Be an
American Buddhist. In Reasons for Living and
Hoping: The Spiritual and Psycho-Social Needs of
Southeast Asian Refugee Children and Youth Resettled
in the United States. Washington, D.C.: The
International Catholic Child Bureau, Inc.

Berry, J. (1987). Acculturation and Psychological Adaptation
among Refugees. In Refugees: The Trauma of Exile.
D. Miserez, ed. Dordrecht: Martinous Nijhoff.

Berval, R. de. (1959). Kingdom of Laos. Limoges, France:
A. Bontemps Co., Ltd.

Bliatout, B. T., et al. (1985). Mental Health and Preservation
Activities Targeted to Southeast Asian Refugees. In
Southeast Asian Mental Health: Treatment, Prevention,
Services, Training and Research. T. Owen, ed.
Washington, D.C.: National Institute of Mental Health.

Blofeld, J. (1971). Mahayana Buddhism in Southeast Asia.
Singapore: Asia Pacific Press.

Buchignani, N. (1988). Towards a Sociology of Indochinese
Canadian Social Organization: A Preliminary
Statement. In Ten Years Later: Indochinese
Communities in Canada. L. J. Dorais, K. B. Chan and
D. M. Indra, eds. Montreal: Canadian Asian Studies
Association.

Burford, G. (1981). Lao Restrospectives: Religion in a Cultural Context. Journal of Refugee Research, vol. 1, pp. 50–58.

Burwell, R. J., P. Hill and J. F. Van Weklin. (1986). Religion and Refugee Resettlement in the United States: A Research Note. Review of Religious Research, vol. 27, pp. 356–366.

Carlin, J. E., and R. Z. Sokoloff,. (1985). Mental Health Treatment Issues for Southeast Asian Refugee Children. In Southeast Asian Mental Health: Treatment, Prevention, Services, Training and Research. T. Owen, ed. Washington, D.C.: National Institute of Mental Health.

CCSDPT. (Committee for the Coordination ofServices to Displaced Persons in Thailand) (1986). The CCSDPT Handbook: Refugee Services in Thailand. Bangkok: CCSDPT.

CEIC
Employment and Immigration Canada, annual reports to parliament on immigration levels.

Chan, K. B. (1987). Unemployment, Social Support and Coping: The Psychosocial Response of Indochinese Refugees to Economic Marginality. In Uprooting, Loss and Adaptation: The Resettlement of Indochinese Refugees in Canada. K. Chan and D. Indra, eds. Ottawa: Canadian Public Health Association.

Chan, K. B. (1990). Getting Through Suffering: Indochinese Refugees in Limbo 15 Years Later. Southeast Journal of Social Science, vol. 18, pp. 1–18.

Chan, K. B., and D. Indra, eds. (1987). Uprooting, Loss and Adaption: The Resettlement of Indochinese Refugees in Canada. Ottawa: Canadian Public Health Association.

Chan, K. B., and L. Lam. (1987a). Community, Kinship and Family in the Chinese Vietnamese Community: Some Enduring Values and Patterns of Interaction. In <u>Uprooting, Loss and Adaptation: The Resettlement of Indochinese Refugees in Canada</u>. K. B. Chan and D. M. Indra, eds. Ottawa: Canadian Public Health Association.

Chan, K. B., and L. Lam. (1987b). Psychological Problems of Chinese Vietnamese Refugee Resettling in Quebec. In <u>Uprooting, Loss and Adaptation: The Resettlement of Indochinese Refugees in Canada</u>. K. B. Chan and D. M. Indra, eds. Ottawa: Canadian Public Health Association.

Chan, K. B., and D. Loveridge. (1987). Refugees "in Transit": Vietnamese in a Refugee Camp in Hong Kong. <u>International Migration Review</u>, vol. 21, pp. 745–758.

Chantavanich, S., and E. B. Reynolds. (1988). <u>Indochinese Refugees: Asylum and Resettlement</u>. Bangkok: Institute of Asian Studies, Chulalongkorn University.

Coedès, G. (1968).<u>The Indianized States of Southeast Asia</u>. Honolulu: East-West Center.

Concominias, G. (1978). A Few Remarks About Thai Political Systems. In <u>Natural Symbols in Southeast Asia</u>, ed. G. Milner. London: School of Oriental and African Studies.

Condominas, G. (1987). In Search of a Vat: The Dai Lu in Internal and the Lao in External Exile. <u>Proceedings of the International Conference on Thai Studies</u>. Canberra:Australian National University.

Copeland, N. (1988). The Southeast Asian Community in Winnipeg. In <u>Ten Years Later: Indochinese Communities in Canada</u>. L. J. Dorais, K. B. Chan and D. Indra, eds. Montreal: Canadian Asian Studies Association.

Coudoux, P. (1985). Wat Lao Buddhavong: a Field Study. Unpublished manuscript, Dept. of Anthropology, American University.

Daniel, V. (1984). Fluid Signs: Being a Person the Tamil Way. Berkeley: University of California Press.

Desan, C. (1983). A Change of Faith for Hmong Refugees. Cultural Survival Quarterly. vol. 7, pp. 50–58.

Dommen, A. (1985). Laos: Keystone of Indochina. Boulder: Westview Press.

Dorais, L.-J. (1987). Language Use and Adaptation. In Uprooting, Loss and Adaptation: The Resettlement of Indochinese Refugees in Canada. K. B. Chan and D. M. Indra, eds. Ottawa: Canadian Public Health Association.

Dorais, L.-J. (1989) Religion and Refugee Adaptation: The Vietnamese in Montreal. CanadianEthnic Studies 21(1):19-29.

Dorais, L.-J., L. Pilon-Lé and N. Huy. (1987). Exile in A Cold Land: A Vietnamese Community in Canada. New Haven: Yale Southeast Asia Studies.

Dorais, L.-J., L. Pilon-Lé (1988). Les communautés cambodgienne et laotienne de Québec. Quebéc: Université Laval, Laboratoire de recherches anthropologiques.

Dumoulin, H. (1976). Buddhism in the Modern World. New York: Macmillan Publishing.

Ebihara, M.. (1985). Khmer. In Refugees in the United States. D. Haines, ed. Westport, Conn.: Greenwood Press.

Engebretson, N. (1983). Stability and Change of Religious Practices of Lao Refugees in Northern Illinois. M. A. thesis, Northern Illinois University, Dekalb.

Engelsmann, F. (1988). Migration and Mental Health. Santé Culture Health. vol. 5, pp. 187–196.

Evans, G. (1990). Lao Peasants Under Socialism. New Haven: Yale University Press.

Geertz, C. (1973). Person, Time and Conduct in Bali. In The Interpretation of Cultures. New York: Basic Books.

Gombrich, R. (1988). Theravada Buddhism. London: Routledge and Kegan Paul.

Gombrich, R., and G. Obeyesekere. (1988). Buddhism Transformed. Princeton, N.J: Princeton University Press.

Gordon, N. (1990). Women's Role in Adaptive Strategies among Laotian Refugee Families in the Toronto Area. York University:North York Faculty of Environmental Studies.

Gosling, D. (1984). Buddhism for Peace. Southeast Asian Journal of Social Science, vol. 12, pp. 59–70.

Griswold, A. B., and P. N. Nagara. (1974). Epigraphic and Historical Series No. 12: Inscription 9. Journal of the Siam Society, vol. 62, No. 1, pp. 89–121.

Gunn, G. (1982). Theravadins and Commissars: The State and National Identity in Laos. In Contemporary Laos. M. Stuart-Fox, ed. New York: St. Martin's Press.

Gyallay-Pap, P. (1989). Reclaiming a Shattered Past: Education for the Displaced Khmer in Thailand. Journal of Refugee Studies, vol. 2, pp. 257–275.

Halpern, J., and S. Pettengill. (1987). The Far World Comes Near: The Kingdom of Laos and Laotian Americans. An Exhibition of Laotian Arts and Culture, April 1987. Augusta Savage Gallery, University of Massachusetts, Amherst.

Hardinge, D. (1988). Statement. Marking Time: The Human Cost of Confinement. CCSDPT Annual Conference Proceedings. Bangkok: CCSDPT.

Hiegel, J. P. (1984). Collaboration With Traditional Healers: Experience In Refugees' Mental Care. International Journal Of Mental Health. Vol. 12, pp. 30–43.

Indochina Resource Centre. (1973). Laos: Showing the Way to Peace. Indochina Chronicle, vol. 29. Washington, D.C., and Berkeley, California.

Indra, D.(1987). Social Science Research on Indochinese Refugees in Canada. In Uprooting, Loss and Adaptation: The Resettlement of Indochinese Refugees in Canada. K. Chan and D. Indra, eds. Ottawa: Canadian Public Health Association.

Indra, D. (1988). An Analysis of the Canadian Private Sponsorship Program for Southeast Asian Refugees. Ethnic Groups, vol. 7, pp. 153–172.

Jambor, P. (1990). Voluntary Repatriation. In Back to a Future. L. Standley, ed. CCSDPT: Bangkok.

Jilek, J. (1988). Marking Time: The Human Cost of Confinement. CCSDPT Conference proceedings, Bangkok.

Johnston, R. (1988). Introductory Remarks. Marking Time: The Human Cost of Confinement. CCSDPT Annual Conference Proceedings. Bangkok: CCSDPT.

Kammerer, C. A. (1988). Of Labels and Laws: Thailand's Resettlement and Repatriation Policies. Cultural Survival Quarterly, vol. 12, pp. 7–12.

Khantipalo, Ven. Thera. (1988). Bodhi Tree. Sydney, Australia: Wat Buddha Dhama, Wisemans Ferry.

Kirsch T. (1973). Feasting and Social Oscilation: Religion and Society in Upland Southeast Asia. Data Paper 92, Southeast Asia Program, Cornell University, Ithaca, New York.

Kuamtou, S. (1981). Lao in Kalihi. In New Immigrants. T. Beng, ed. New York: Pilgrim Press.

Lafont, P. B. (1982). Buddhism in Contemporary Laos. In Contemporary Laos. M. Stuart Fox, ed. New York: St. Martin's Press.

Lanphier, C. M. (1987). Indochinese Resettlement: Cost and Adaption in Canada, the United States, and France. In Refugees: A Third World Dilemma. J. Rogge, ed. Totowa, N. J.: Rowman and Littlefield.

LeBar, F., and A. Suddard. (1960). Laos: Its People, Its Society, Its Culture. New Haven: HRAF Press.

Lewis, R. E. M., W. Fraser and P. J. Pecora. (1988). Religiosity Among Indochinese Refugees in Utah. Journal for the Scientific Study of Religion, vol. 27, pp. 272–283.

Luangpraseut, K. (1989). Keynote Speaker. In Reasons for Living and Hoping: The Spiritual and Psycho-Social Needs of Southeast Asian Refugee Children and Youth Resettled in the United States. Washington, D.C.: The International Catholic Child Bureau, Inc.

McAteer, M. (1988). New Attitudes Make it Easier for Buddhism to Flourish Today. Toronto Star. June 4.

McLellan, J. (1987). The Role of Buddhism in Managing Ethnic Identity Among Tibetans in Lindsay, Ontario. Canadian Ethnic Studies, vol. 19, pp. 63–76.

McLellan, J. (1992). Hermit Crabs and Refugees: Adaptive Strategies of Vietnamese Buddhists in Toronto. In The Quality of Life in Southeast Asia. B. Matthews (ed.) Montreal: Canadian Asian Studies Association.

Mollica, R. F. (1990). Communities of Confinement: An International Plan for Relieving the Mental Health Crisis in the Thai-Khmer Border Camps. Social Science, Vol. 18, pp. 132–152.

Morreale, D., ed. (1988). Buddhist America: Centers, Retreats, Practices. Sante Fe: John Muir Publications.

Muecke, M. (1987). Resettled Refugees' Reconstruction of Identity: Lao in Seattle. Urban Anthropology, vol. 16, nos. 3–4, pp. 273–289.

Muir, K. (1988). The Strongest Part of the Family: A Study of Lao Refugee Women in Columbus, Ohio. New York: AMS Press.

Muntarbhorn, V. (1987). Statement at CCSDPT Annual Conference Proceedings. CCSDPT Conference, July 1987, Bangkok.

Nakavachara, N. and J. Rogge. (1987). Thailand's Refugee Experience. In Refugees: A Third World Dilemma. J. Rogge, ed. Totowa, N. J.: Rowman and Littlefield.

Neuwirth, G. and J. R. Rogge. (1988). Canada and the Indochinese Refugees. In Indochinese Refugees. S. Chantavanich and B. Reynolds, eds. Bangkok: Institute of Asian Studies, Chulalongkorn University.

Ngaosyvathn, M. (1990). Individual Soul, National Identity: The Baci-Sou Khuan of the Lao. Sojourn. vol. 5, pp. 283–307.

O'Connor, R. (1985). Centers and Sanctity, Regions and Religion: Varieties of Tai Buddhism. Paper presented at the Annual Meeting of the American Anthropological Association, Washington, D.C.

Owen, T. C., ed. (1985). Southeast Asian Mental Health: Treatment, Prevention, Services, Training and Research. Washington, D.C.: National Institute of Mental Health.

Placzek, J. (1987). Definitions and Associations of being a Lao-Canadian in Vancouver. Paper presented at the Canadian Council for Southeast Asian Studies, Saskatoon.

Pongsapit, A. and N. Chongwattana. (1988). The Refugee Situation in Thailand. In Indochinese Refugees. S. Chantavanich and B. Reynolds, eds. Bangkok: Institute of Asian Studies, Chulalongkorn University.

Rabé, P. (1990). Voluntary Repatriation: The Case of Hmong in Ban Vinai. Indochinese Refugee Information Center (IRIC). Bangkok: Institute for Asian Studies, Chulalongkorn University.

Rajah, A. (1990). Orientalism, Commensurability and the Construction of Lao Identity: A Comment on the Notion of Lao Identity. Sojourn, vol. 5, pp. 308–333.

Rajavaramuni, P. (1984). Thai Buddhism in the Buddhist World. Bangkok: Mahachulalongkorn Buddhist University.

Ratannapanna, P. (1968). The Sheaf of Garlands of the Epochs of the Conqueror. N. A. Jayawickrama, trans. PTS Translation series. London: Luzak and Co.

Reynolds, F. (1978). Rituals and Social Hierarchy: An Aspect of Traditional Religion in Buddhist Laos. The Holy Emerald Jewel: Some Aspects of Buddhist Symbolism and Political Legitimation in Thailand and Laos. In Religion and Legitimation of Power in Thailand, Laos and Burma, B. Smith, ed. Chambersburg, Penn.: Anima Books.

Rumbaut, R. D. (1985). Mental Health and the Refugee Experience: A Comparative Study of Southeast Asian Refugees. In Southeast Asian Mental Health: Treatment, Prevention, Services, Training and Research. T. Owen, ed. Washington, D.C.: National Institute of Mental Health.

Rumbaut, R. et al. (1988). The Politics of Migrant Health Care: A Comparative Study of Mexican Immigrants and Indochinese Refugees. Research in the Sociology of Health Care, vol. 7, pp. 143–202.

Rynearson, A. M., and P. A. DeVoe. (1984). Refugee Women in a Vertical Village: Lowland Laotians in St. Louis. Social Thought, vol. 10, pp. 33–48.

Samart, M. (1992). The Consequences Of Economic and Political Background for the Resettlement of Laotian Refugee Women and Men in Toronto. Faculty of Environmental Studies, York University: North York.

Simon-Barouh, I. (1983). The Cambodians In Rennes: A Study of Inter-Ethnic Relations. Urban Anthropology, vol. 12, pp. 1– 28.

Sivaraksa, S. (1986). A Buddhist Vision for Renewing Society. Bangkok: Tienivan Publishing House, Ltd.

Spiro, M. (1970). Buddhism and Society. New York: Harper and Row.

Smith, D. E. (1971). Religion, Politics and Social Change in the Third World. New York: Free Press.

Stuart-Fox, Martin. (1981). Socialist Construction and National Security in Laos. Bulletin of Concerned Asian Scholars, vol. 13, pp. 61–71.

Stuart-Fox, M. (1982). Contemporary Laos: Studies in the Politics and Society of the Lao People's Democratic Republic. New York: St. Martin's Press.

Stuart-Fox, M. and R. Bucknell. (1982). Politicization of the Buddhist Sangha in Laos. Journal of Southeast Asian Studies, vol. 13, pp. 60–80.

Stuart-Fox, M. (1983). Marxism and Theravada Buddhism: The Legitimization of Political Authority in Laos. Pacific Affairs, vol. 56, pp 428–454.

Stuart-Fox, M. (1986). Laos: Politics, Economics and Society. London: Frances Pinter.

Suksamran, S. (1977). Political Buddhism in Southeast Asia. London: C. Hurst and Company.

Suzuki, D. (1956). Zen Buddhism. Garden City, N. J.: Doubleday.

TAC. (1985). Newsletter, March 15, 1985, Thai Association of Canada

Tambiah, S. J. (1970). Buddhism and the Spirit Cults of Northeast Thailand. Cambridge: Cambridge University Press.

Tambiah, S. J. (1984). The Buddhist Saints of the Forest and the Cult of Amulets. Cambridge: Cambridge University Press.

Terweil, B. (1975). Monks and Magic: An Analysis of Religious Ceremonies in Central Thailand. Lund, Sweden: Student-litteratur. Scandinavian Institute of Asian Studies.

UNHCR, Bangkok
    Refers to distribution of data from UNHCR, Bangkok

Uparatana, Venerable K. (1989). Perspective of a Buddhist Monk. In Reasons for Living and Hoping: The Spiritual and Psycho-Social Needs of Southeast Asian Refugee Children and Youth Resettled in the United States. Washington, D.C.: The International Catholic Child Bureau, Inc.

Van Esterik, J. (1977). Cultural Interpretation of Canonical Paradox: Lay Meditation in a Central Thai Village. Ph.D. dissertation, University of Illinois, Urbana.

Van Esterik, J. (1978). Construction of Relief and Ritual Time in a Central Thai Village. Paper presented at the Canadian Society for Sociology and Anthropology, London, Ontario, June.

Van Esterik, J. (1985). Lao. In Refugees in the United States. D. Hines, ed. Westport, Conn.: Greenwood Press.

Van Esterik, P. (1973). Thai Tonsura Ceremonies: A Reinterpretation of Brahmanic Ritual in Thailand. Journal of the Steward Anthropological Society, vol. 4, No. 2, pp. 79–121.

Van Esterik, P. (1980a). Cultural Factors Affecting the Adjustment of Southeast Asian Refugees. In Southeast Asian Exodus: From Tradition to Settlement. E. Tepper, ed. Ottawa: Canadian Asian Studies Association.

Van Esterik, P. (1980b). Royal Style in Village Contact: Towards a Model of Interaction between Royalty and Commoner. Essays in Thai Administrative, Economic, and Social History. C. Wilson, C. Smith and G. Smith, eds. Contributions to Asian Studies, vol XV, 102-117.

Van Esterik, P. (1981). In-Home Sponsorship for Southeast Asian Refugees: A Preliminary Assessment. Journal of Refugee Resettlement, vol. 1, no. 2, pp. 18–26.

Van Esterik, P. (1982). Interpreting Cosmology: Guardian Spirits in Thai Buddhism. Anthropos, vol. 77, pp. 1–15.

Viviani, N. (1988). Australia and the Indochinese Refugees. In Indochinese Refugees: Asylum and Resettlement. S. Chantavanich and B. Reynolds, eds., Bangkok: Institute of Asian Studies, Chulalongkorn University.

Wedel, Y. with P. Wedel. (1987) Radical Though, Thai Mind. Assumption Business Administration College, Bangkok.

148

Wells, K. E. (1960). Thai Buddhism. Bangkok: Police Printing Press.

Westermeyer, J. and R. Wintrob. (1979). Folk Explanations of Mental Illness in Rural Laos. American Journal of Psychiatry, vol. 136, pp. 901-905.

Williams, C. (1989). Mental Health Perspective. In Reasons for Living and Hoping: The Spiritual and Psycho-Social Needs of Southeast Asian Refugee Children and Youth Resettled in the United States. Washington, D.C.: The International Catholic Child Bureau, Inc.

Winland, D. (1992). The Role of Religious Affiliation in Refugee Resettlement: The Case Of Hmong Mennonites. Canadian Ethnic Studies, vol. 24, 96-119.

Woon, Y.-F. (1987). The Mode of Refugee Sponsorship and the Socio-Economic Adaptation of Vietnamese in Victoria: A Three Year Perspective. In Uprooting, Loss and Adaptation: The Resettlement of Indochinese Refugees in Canada. K. B. Chan and D. M. Indra. eds. Ottawa: Canadian Public Health Association.

Woon, Y. -F., et al. (1988). Loose Sand: The Ethnic Vietnamese and Sino-Vietnamese Community in Greater Victoria (1980-1985). In Ten Years Later: IndoChinese Communities in Canada. Canadian Asian Studies Association, Montreal.

Zaharlick, A., and J. Brainard. (1988). Fertility, Transition and the Changing Status of Laotian Refugee Women. Paper prepared at the Annual Meeting of the American Anthropological Association, Phoenix, Arizona.